A farewell book from one of the giants of our generation. John Stott outlines eight key aspects of discipleship with piercing clarity. Especially moving and profound are his final chapters on dependence and death.

Amy Boucher Pye, editor and columnist

Like a favourite great-uncle's legacy, this little collection of farewell messages from a great man of God and radical disciple of Jesus bequeaths to us some precious treasures – warm appeals to distinctive Christlike maturity, challenging contemporary calls to ecological concern, simplicity and balance, priceless wisdom from an elderly saint about dependence and dying – and all delivered with his customary economy, clarity and faithfulness to Scripture. Such mature reflections are surely priceless.

Richard Coekin, Senior Pastor of the Co-Mission Initiative, SW London

I have always felt a little sad at the thought that when Uncle John eventually goes, he will take so much with him: the gathered experience of a life truly well lived, as well as the intellectual capital he has banked for the sake of the kingdom of God. How could he ever possibly distil the essence of this lifetime's worth of wisdom, so that we may continue to draw inspiration and learn from this great teacher?

But he has achieved the seemingly impossible: he has captured the essence of what it means, to him, to be a radical disciple, and written this for us with a light touch; with a sense that THIS is the heart, that it doesn't have to be made perplexingly complex, or intimidating in an intellectual way; that having understood profoundly, the joy of his life's work is to communicate simply.

And that simple communication is manifested most clearly and effectively in the idea of the radical, and simple, life. I have not read a better or more compelling short section on how to live.

Here we have a snapshot of what Uncle John believes is the gold; and I, for one, will enter the next phase of my own discipleship much richer as a result. I believe it's not only a great achievement to write so succinctly, given the sheer breadth and depth of his life's work – it is also a vivid demonstration of the simple tension at the heart of the gospel: that we are challenged to carry the cross daily, and walk the narrow path, and yet simultaneously we are promised that the yoke of Christ is easy, and the burden is light.

I've always wanted to enter more fully into what Eugene Peterson calls 'the unforced rhythms of grace' (Matthew 11). This is the book I will turn to, repeatedly, for help.

Brian Draper is associate lecturer in culture at the London Institute for Contemporary Christianity, author of Spiritual Intelligence, *and runs a small enterprise called Echosounder, nurturing spiritual intelligence in leaders.*

For forty years John Stott has been teaching me what it means to be a follower of Christ by carefully studying the Scriptures and applying them to the various issues I face, and often to issues I should face and don't. He does just that in this his last book. This book shows that at the age of eighty-eight my mentor still has the passion for truth and devotion to Christ that he had when I encountered him all those years ago. What a wonderful way to say, 'Farewell' to his readers. I especially recommend this book to young believers who wonder whether it is possible to live the Christian life with integrity, especially if one is famous. John Stott's greatest impact on me has been the way his life has modelled Christian character. I think this combination of integrity in life and teaching is what has made him one of the most influential individuals in recent history. Read this book, not only to be instructed by penetrative biblical wisdom on what discipleship means in today's world, but also in order to be inspired by the life and teaching of one who is finishing well.

Ajith Fernando, National Director, Youth for Christ, Sri Lanka

Who better than John Stott, with his life-long commitment to living as a follower of Jesus, to issue this timely call to take Jesus' teaching seriously? The world desperately needs to see that there are other ways to live, and all too often Christians tend to conform to the patterns of society rather than demonstrating the distinctiveness that Jesus asks of us. If heeded, this call could revitalize the witness of the church.

John Grayston, Director of Theology, Scripture Union

For over sixty years John Stott's penetrating and profoundly biblical insights have thrown light on many of the challenging issues that have faced the global church. This book brings all those years of experience, reflection and study to bear on a series of questions that he believes we are neglecting. That alone should cause us to listen with particular care even if he didn't tell us that this is to be his final published message. Furthermore, these pages give us a rare and personal glimpse of the sacrificial discipleship that has marked his life so deeply – that is one more reason for us to learn what we can from a truly exceptional leader.

Peter Harris, founder of A Rocha

We enthusiastically recommend this unique book, filled with fascinating recollections amassed over a lifetime of wisdom, combined with insightful scholarship and a deep love for the body of Christ across the world.

Frog and Amy Orr-Ewing, speakers and authors

The Radical Disciple is a beautifully straightforward clarion call to re-establish the truly converted life within a contemporary Christian sub-culture diluted by the self-centredness of the age. This is John Stott at his thoughtful, reflective best. His thinking is succinct, incisive and truly describes how authentic followers of Jesus live. Jesus doesn't simply tweak our lives, but rebuilds them from the foundations up. We have neglected the challenge of that radical, converting work. Here is a book that inspires us to embrace deep conversion. Read this and discover what a wholehearted follower of Jesus is like.

Dominic Smart, minister, Gilcomston South Church of Scotland, Aberdeen

This book is faithfully biblical, deeply engaging, firmly challenging and profoundly moving – a characteristically masterful survey of a subject we all too easily neglect. I can think of no better teacher on this theme than John Stott, whose lifetime of personal commitment to radical discipleship shines out from every page.

David Stone, Team Rector of Newbury

The
Radical
Disciple

John Stott

The Radical Disciple

Wholehearted Christian Living

ivp

INTER-VARSITY PRESS
Norton Street, Nottingham NG7 3HR, England
Email: ivp@ivpbooks.com
Website: www.ivpbooks.com

First published 2010
Reprinted 2010 (twice)

British Library Cataloguing in Publication Data
A catalogue record for this book is available from the British Library.

ISBN: 978–1–84474–421–3

Set in Adobe Garamond
Typeset in Great Britain by CRB Associates, Potterhanworth, Lincolnshire
Printed in Great Britain by Ashford Colour Press, Gosport, Hampshire

*Inter-Varsity Press publishes Christian books that are true to the Bible and that
communicate the gospel, develop discipleship and strengthen the church for its
mission in the world.*

*Inter-Varsity Press is closely linked with the Universities and Colleges Christian
Fellowship, a student movement connecting Christian Unions in universities and
colleges throughout Great Britain, and a member movement of the International
Fellowship of Evangelical Students. Website: www.uccf.org.uk*

CONTENTS

ACKNOWLEDGMENTS

Because the writing of this book was begun, continued and ended under the hospitable roof of the College of St Barnabas, my first thanks must go to its personnel, and to its warden and his wife, Howard and Lynne Such, to its residents and patients, to the nursing, caring, administrative, catering and cleaning staffs, since together they have created a rich Christian community of worship and fellowship, a context congenial to thinking and writing. When sometimes I have been preoccupied with these activities, I must have seemed an anti-social creature, but they have understood and forgiven me.

Another community to which I am indebted is that of St John's Church, Felbridge; to their vicar Stephen Bowen, his wife Mandy, and their church wardens Anne Butler and Malcolm Francis. When I have felt strong enough, they have kindly arranged for me to be transported there and back on Sundays. They knew that a book was brewing and encouraged me along the way.

I greatly appreciate the editorial skill of David Stone, assisted by Eleanor Trotter, while other individuals who have contributed to the text include John Wyatt and Sheila Moore, both of whom have enriched Chapter 7 from their personal experiences. Peter Harris and Chris Wright have helped me with Chapter 4, while Grace Lam has given me vital information about her late husband's ministry (Chapter 5).

It has been a regular encouragement to receive a fortnightly visit from my nieces Caroline and Sarah, and my friend Phillip Herbert almost as often. Others have worked behind the scenes for me, for instance John Smith, who has patiently surfed the net for me.

Last but not least, Frances Whitehead has managed to maintain her weekly visits and so keep up with the endless stream of e-mails which she handles with extraordinary skill, together with this manuscript.

John Stott
Easter 2009

PREFACE:
DISCIPLES OR CHRISTIANS?

Let me explain and justify the title of this book, *The Radical Disciple*.

First, why 'disciple'?

It comes as a surprise to many people to discover that the followers of Jesus Christ are called 'Christian' only three times in the New Testament.

The most significant occurrence is Luke's comment that it was in Syrian Antioch that Jesus' disciples were first called 'Christians' (Acts 11:26). Antioch was known to be an international community. Consequently its church was an international community too, and it was appropriate that its members were called 'Christians' in order to indicate that their ethnic differences were overcome by their common allegiance to Christ.

The other two occurrences of the word 'Christian' supply evidence that it was beginning to come into common currency. So when Paul was on trial before King Agrippa and challenged him directly, Agrippa cried out to Paul, 'Do you think that in such a short time you can persuade me to be a Christian?' (Acts 26:28).

Then the apostle Peter, whose first letter was written against the background of growing persecution, found it necessary to distinguish between those who suffered 'as a criminal' and those who suffered 'as a Christian' (1 Peter 4:16); that is, because they belonged to Christ. Both words (Christian and disciple) imply a relationship with Jesus, although perhaps 'disciple' is the stronger of the two because it inevitably implies the relationship of pupil to teacher. During his three years of public ministry the Twelve were disciples before they were apostles, and as disciples they were under the instruction of their teacher and lord.

One wishes in some ways that the word 'disciple' had continued into the following centuries, so that Christians were self-consciously disciples of Jesus, and took seriously their responsibility to be 'under discipline'.

My concern in this book is that we who claim to be disciples of the Lord Jesus will not provoke him to say again: 'Why do you call me, "Lord, Lord," and do not do what I say?' (Luke 6:46). For genuine discipleship is wholehearted discipleship, and this is where my next word comes in.

So, secondly, why 'radical'? Since this is the adjective I am using to describe our discipleship, it is important to indicate the sense in which I am using it.

The English word 'radical' is derived from the Latin word *radix*, a root. Originally it seems to have been applied as a political label to people like the nineteenth-century politician William Cobbett and their extreme, liberal and reformist views. But from this it came to be applied generally to those whose opinions went to the roots and who were thoroughgoing in their commitment.

We are now ready to put the noun and the adjective together and to ask our third question, namely why 'radical disciple'? The answer is obvious. There are different levels of commitment in the Christian community. Jesus himself illustrated this in what happened to the seeds he describes in the Parable of the Sower.[1] The difference between the seeds lay in the kind of soil which received them. Of the seed sown on rocky soil Jesus said, 'It had no root.'

Our common way of avoiding radical discipleship is to be selective; choosing those areas in which commitment suits us and staying away from those areas in which it will be costly. But because Jesus is Lord, we have no right to pick and choose the areas in which we will submit to his authority.

> Jesus is worthy to receive
> > Honour and power divine.
> And blessings more than we can give
> > Be Lord for ever thine.[2]

So my purpose in this book is to consider eight characteristics of Christian discipleship which are often neglected and yet deserve to be taken seriously.

Chapter 1

NON-CONFORMITY

The first characteristic of the radical disciple which I bring before you I will call 'non-conformity'. Let me explain why.

The church has a double responsibility in relation to the world around us. On the one hand we are to live, serve and witness in the world. On the other hand we are to avoid becoming contaminated by the world. So we are neither to seek to preserve our holiness by escaping from the world nor to sacrifice our holiness by conforming to the world.

Escapism and conformism are thus both forbidden to us. This is one of the major themes of the whole Bible, namely that God is calling out a people for himself and is summoning us to be different from everybody else. 'Be holy,' he says repeatedly to his people, 'because I am holy' (e.g. Leviticus 11:45; 1 Peter 1:15–16).

We are neither to seek to preserve our holiness by escaping from the world nor to sacrifice our holiness by conforming to the world.

This foundational theme recurs in all four of the main sections of Scripture: the law, the prophets, the teaching of Jesus, and the teaching of the apostles. Let me give you an example from each. First, the law. God said to his people through Moses:

> You must not do as they do in Egypt, where you used to live, and you must not do as they do in the land of Canaan, where I am bringing you. Do not follow their practices. You must obey my laws and be careful to follow my decrees. I am the LORD your God (Leviticus 18:3–4).

Similarly, God's criticism of his people through the prophet Ezekiel is that 'you have not followed my decrees

or kept my laws but have conformed to the standards of
the nations around you' (Ezekiel 11:12).

It is the same in the New Testament. In the Sermon on
the Mount Jesus spoke of the hypocrites and the pagans,
and added: 'Do not be like them' (Matthew 6:8). Finally
the apostle Paul wrote to the Romans: 'Do not conform
to the pattern of this world, but be transformed by the
renewing of your mind' (Romans 12:2).

Here then is God's call to a radical discipleship, to a
radical non-conformity to the surrounding culture. It is
a call to develop a Christian counterculture, a call to
engagement without compromise.

So what are the contemporary trends which threaten to
swallow us up, and which we must resist? We will consider
four. First, the challenge of *pluralism*. Pluralism affirms that
every 'ism' has its own independent validity and an equal
right to our respect. It therefore rejects Christian claims to
finality and uniqueness, and condemns as sheer arrogance
the attempt to convert anybody (let alone everybody) to
what it sees as merely our opinions.

How then should we respond to the spirit of pluralism?
With great humility, I hope, and with no hint of personal
superiority. But we must continue to affirm the uniqueness
and finality of Jesus Christ. For he is unique in his incarnation (the one and only God-man); unique in his atonement
(only he has died for the sins of the world); and unique in
his resurrection (only he has conquered death). And since
in no other person but Jesus of Nazareth did God first

become human (in his birth), then bear our sins (in his death), and then triumph over death (in his resurrection), he is uniquely competent to save sinners. Nobody else possesses his qualifications. So we may talk about Alexander the Great, Charles the Great and Napoleon the Great, but not Jesus the Great. He is not the Great – he is the Only. There is nobody like him. He has no rival and no successor.

A second widespread secular trend which Christian disciples have to resist is that of *materialism*. Materialism is not simply an acceptance of the reality of the material world. If that were the case, all Christians would be materialists, since we believe that God has created the material world and made its blessings available to us. God has also affirmed the material order through the incarnation and resurrection of his Son, in the water of baptism and the bread and wine of Holy Communion. It is no wonder that William Temple described Christianity as the most material of all religions. But it is not materialistic.

For materialism is a preoccupation with material things, which can smother our spiritual life. But Jesus told us not to store up treasure on earth and warned us against covetousness. So did the apostle Paul, urging us instead to develop a lifestyle of simplicity, generosity and content-ment, drawing on his own experience of having learned to be content whatever the circumstances (Philippians 4:11).

Paul added that 'godliness with contentment is great gain' (1 Timothy 6:6) and then went on to explain that 'we brought nothing into the world, and we can take nothing out of it'. Perhaps he was consciously echoing Job who said: 'Naked I came from my mother's womb, and naked I shall depart' (Job 1:21). In other words, life on earth is a brief pilgrimage between two moments of nakedness. So we would be wise to travel light. We shall take nothing with us. (I will say more about materialism in Chapter 5.)

The third contemporary trend which threatens us and to which we must not surrender is the insidious spirit of *ethical relativism*.

All round us moral standards are slipping. This is certainly so in the West. People are confused as to whether there are any absolutes left. Relativism has permeated culture and is seeping into the church.

There is no sphere in which this relativism is more obvious than in that of sexual ethics and the sexual revolution which has taken place since the 1960s. It used to be universally accepted (at least wherever Judeo-Christian ethics were taken seriously) that marriage is a monogamous, heterosexual, loving and lifelong union, and the only God-given context for sexual intimacy. But now, even in some churches, co-habitation without marriage is widely practised, dispensing with that commitment which is essential to authenticate marriage, while same-sex partnerships are promoted as a legitimate alternative to heterosexual marriage.

Over against these trends Jesus Christ calls his disciples to obedience and to conform to his standards. It is sometimes claimed that Jesus did not speak about these things. But he did. He quoted both Genesis 1:27 ('At the beginning the Creator "made them male and female"') and Genesis 2:24 ('A man will leave his father and mother and be united to his wife, and the two will become one flesh') as giving the biblical definition of marriage. And after quoting these Scriptures Jesus gave them his own personal endorsement, saying 'what God has joined together, let no-one separate' (Matthew 19:4–6).

This viewpoint was critically evaluated by the distinguished American moral and social philosopher Abraham Edel (1908–2007), whose first major book was entitled *Ethical Judgment*, and subtitled 'the use of science in ethics'.[1]

'Morality is ultimately arbitrary,' he wrote, and went on with a piece of popular doggerel:

It all depends on where you are,
It all depends on who you are,
It all depends on what you feel,
It all depends on how you feel.
It all depends on how you're raised,
It all depends on what is praised,
What's right today is wrong tomorrow,
Joy in France, in England sorrow.
It all depends on point of view,
Australia or Timbuctoo,
In Rome do as the Romans do.
If tastes just happen to agree
Then you have morality.

> But where there are conflicting trends,
> It all depends, it all depends . . .

But radical Christian disciples must disagree. To be sure, we are not to be completely rigid in our ethical decision-making, but seek sensitively to apply biblical principles in each situation. Fundamental to Christian behaviour is the lordship of Jesus Christ. 'Jesus is Lord' remains the basis of our life.

So the fundamental question before the church is who is Lord? Is the church the lord of Jesus Christ, so that it has liberty to edit and manipulate, accepting what it likes and rejecting what it dislikes? Or is Jesus Christ our Teacher and our Lord, so that we believe and obey his teaching?

He still says to us, 'Why do you call me, "Lord, Lord," and do not do what I say?' (Luke 6:46). To confess Jesus as Lord but not obey him is to build our lives on a foundation of sand. Again, 'Whoever has my commands and keeps them is the one who loves me,' he said in the upper room (John 14:21).

Here then are two cultures and two value systems, two standards and two lifestyles. On the one side there is the fashion of the world around us; on the other side is the revealed, good and pleasing will of God.

Radical disciples have little difficulty in making their choice.

We come now to a fourth contemporary trend, which is the challenge of *narcissism*.

Narcissus (in Greek mythology) was a handsome young man who caught sight of his reflection in a pond, fell in love with his own image, toppled into the water and drowned. So 'narcissism' is an excessive love for oneself, an unbounded admiration of 'self'.

In the 1970s narcissism found expression in the Human Potential Movement, which laid emphasis on the need for self-actualization. In the 1980s and 1990s the New Age Movement jumped on the bandwagon of the Human Potential Movement. Shirley MacLaine could be called its high priestess and she was infatuated with herself. According to her the good news goes like this:

> I know that I exist; therefore I am.
> I know the god force exists; therefore it is.
> Since I am a part of that force, I am that I am.

It sounds like a deliberate parody of God's revelation of himself to Moses: 'I AM WHO I AM' (Exodus 3:14).

So the New Age Movement calls us to look inside ourselves, to explore ourselves, for the solution to our problems is within. We do not need a saviour to come to us from somewhere else; we can be our own saviour.

Unfortunately, some of this teaching has permeated the church, with some Christians urging that we must not only love God and our neighbour, but we must also love ourselves. But no, this is surely a mistake for three reasons. First, Jesus spoke of 'the first and great commandment' and of 'the second', but did not mention a third. Secondly, self-love is one of the signs of the last days (2 Timothy 3:2). Thirdly, the meaning of *agape* love is the sacrifice of oneself in the service of others. Sacrificing oneself in the service of oneself is clearly nonsense! What then should our attitude be to ourselves? It is a combination of self-affirmation and self-denial – affirming everything in us which comes to us from our creation and redemption, and denying everything which can be traced to the fall.

It is a great relief to turn away from an unhealthy preoccupation with oneself to the healthy commandments of God (united and reinforced by Jesus), to love God with our whole being and to love our neighbour as ourself. For God intends his church to be a community of love, a worshipping and serving community.

Everybody knows that love is the greatest thing in the world, and Christians know why. It is because God is love.

The thirteenth-century Spanish courtier, Raymond Lull (a missionary to Muslims in North Africa), wrote that 'he who loves not, lives not'. For living is loving, and without love the human personality disintegrates. That is why everybody is looking for the authentic relationships of love.

Looking back, we have considered four major secular trends which threaten to engulf the Christian community. In the face of these we are all called, not to feeble-minded conformity, but to radical non-conformity. Over against the challenge of pluralism, we are to be a community of truth, standing up for the uniqueness of Jesus Christ. Over against the challenge of materialism, we are to be a community of simplicity and pilgrimage. Over against the challenge of relativism, we are to be a community of obedience. Over against the challenge of narcissism, we are to be a community of love.

We are not to be like reeds shaken by the wind, bowing down before gusts of public opinion, but as immovable as rocks in a mountain stream. We are not to be like fish floating with the stream (for 'only dead fish swim with the current', as Malcolm Muggeridge put it), but to swim against the stream, even against the cultural mainstream. We are not to be like chameleons, lizards which change their colour according to their surroundings, but to stand out visibly against our surroundings.

We are not to be like reeds shaken
by the wind, bowing down
before gusts of public opinion,
but as immovable as rocks
in a mountain stream.

What then are Christians to be like if we are not to be like reeds, dead fish or chameleons? Is God's word entirely negative, simply telling us to avoid being moulded into the shape of those in the world around us? No. It is positive. We are to be like Christ, 'conformed to the image of God's Son' (Romans 8:29). And that brings us to the next chapter.

Chapter 2

CHRISTLIKENESS

In April 2007 I celebrated my 86th birthday and took the opportunity to announce my retirement from active public ministry. Although I declined all subsequent speaking engagements, I already had in my diary an invitation to give an address at the Keswick Convention[1] that July. This chapter is based on the text of that last address.

I remember vividly the major question which perplexed me (and my friends) as a young Christian. It was this: What is God's purpose for his people? Granted we had been converted, but what next?

Of course we knew the famous statement of the Westminster Shorter Catechism, that 'Man's chief end is to glorify God and to enjoy him for ever'. We also toyed with a yet briefer statement of only five words such as 'love God, love your neighbour'.

But neither seemed wholly satisfactory. So I want to share with you where my mind has come to rest as I approach the end of my pilgrimage on earth. It is this: God wants his people to become like Christ, for Christlikeness is the will of God for the people of God.

I propose first, to lay down the biblical basis for the call to Christlikeness; second, to give some New Testament examples; and third, to draw some practical conclusions.

THE BIBLICAL BASIS OF THE CALL TO CHRISTLIKENESS

This basis is not a single text, for the basis is more substantial than can be summed up in one text. The basis consists of three texts which we will do well to hold together: Romans 8:29, 2 Corinthians 3:18 and 1 John 3:2.

The first text is Romans 8:29: God has 'predestined [his people] to be conformed to the image of his Son'. When Adam fell, he lost much (though not all) of the divine image in which he had been created. But God has restored it in Christ. Conformity to the image of God means to be like Jesus, and Christlikeness is the eternal predestinating purpose of God.

The second text is 2 Corinthians 3:18: 'We all, who with unveiled faces contemplate [or reflect] the Lord's glory, are being transformed [or changed] into his image, with ever-increasing glory, which comes from the Lord, who is the Spirit.'

The perspective has changed – from the past to the present; from God's eternal predestination to his present transformation of us by the Holy Spirit; from God's eternal purpose to make us like Christ, to his historical work by his Spirit to transform us into the image of Christ.

The third text is 1 John 3:2: 'Dear friends, now we are children of God, and what we will be has not yet been made known. But we know that when Christ appears, we shall be like him, for we shall see him as he is.' And if God is working to this end, it is no wonder he calls us to cooperate with him. 'Follow me,' he says. 'Imitate me.'

Many of us have heard of a book entitled *The Imitation of Christ* which was written in the early fifteenth century by Thomas à Kempis. So many hundreds of thousands of editions and translations have been published that, after the Bible, it is probably the world's best-seller. It is not actually about imitating Christ for its contents are more varied than this. But it got its title from the book's first words, and its enormous popularity is an indication of the importance of its topic.

So, returning now to 1 John 3:2: We don't know, and we do know; we don't know in any detail what we shall be, but we do know that we will be like Christ. And there's really no need for us to know any more. We are content with the glorious truth that we will be with Christ and like Christ.

Here then are three perspectives (past, present and future) which are all pointing in the same direction: God's *eternal* purpose (we have been predestined . . .); God's *historical* purpose (we are being changed, transformed by the Holy Spirit); and God's final *eschatological* purpose (we will be like him . . .). These all combine towards the same end of Christlikeness, for Christlikeness is the purpose of God for the people of God.

If we claim to be Christian,
we must be like Christ.

Having established the biblical basis, that Christlikeness is the purpose of God for the people of God, I want now to move on to illustrate this truth with a number of New Testament examples. But first, a general statement from 1 John 2:6: 'whoever claims to live in him must live as Jesus did'. If we claim to be Christian, we must be like Christ.

SOME NEW TESTAMENT EXAMPLES

We are to be like Christ in his incarnation
Some may immediately recoil with horror from such an

idea. 'Surely,' you may say, 'the incarnation was an altogether unique event and cannot be imitated?'

The answer is 'yes and no'. It is 'yes' in the sense that the Son of God took our humanity to himself in Jesus of Nazareth, once and for all and never to be repeated, but 'no' in the sense that we are all called to follow the example of his great humility. So Paul could write in Philippians 2:5–8:

Have the same attitude of mind Christ Jesus had:

who, being in very nature God,
    did not consider equality with God something
        to be used to his own advantage;
rather, he made himself nothing
    by taking the very nature of a servant,
    being made in human likeness.
And being found in appearance as a human being,
    he humbled himself
    by becoming obedient to death – even death on
        a cross!

We are to be like Christ in his service

We move on now from his incarnation to his life of service. So come with me to the upper room where he spent his last evening with his disciples. During supper he took off his outer garments, tied a towel round him, poured water into a basin and washed his disciples' feet. When he had finished, he resumed his place and said: 'Now that I, your Lord and Teacher, have washed your feet, you also should wash one another's feet. I have set you an example that you should do as I have done for you' (John 13:14–15).

Some Christians take Jesus' command literally and sometimes have a foot-washing ceremony in their Lord's Supper. And they may be right. But most also transpose his command culturally. That is, just as Jesus performed what in his culture was the work of a slave, so we in our cultures must regard no task too menial or degrading to undertake.

We are to be like Christ in his love

As Paul wrote: 'Live a life of love, just as Christ loved us and gave himself up for us as a fragrant offering and sacrifice to God' (Ephesians 5:2). To 'live a life of love' is a command that all our behaviour should be characterized by love, but 'gave himself' for us is a clear reference to the cross. So Paul is urging us to be like Christ in his death; to love with Calvary love.

Do you see what is happening? Paul is urging us to be like the Christ of the incarnation, the Christ of the foot-washing, and the Christ of the cross.

These events in the life of Christ indicate clearly what Christlikeness means in practice. For example, in this very chapter Paul urges husbands to love their wives as Christ loved the church and gave himself for her (Ephesians 5:25).

We are to be like Christ in his patient endurance

In this next example we consider the teaching, not of Paul but of Peter. Every chapter of Peter's first letter contains an allusion to suffering for Christ, for the background of the letter is the beginnings of persecution.

In chapter 2 in particular, Peter urges Christian slaves (if punished unjustly) to bear it, not to repay evil for evil (1 Peter 2:18). We have been called to this because Christ also suffered, leaving us an example so that we may follow in his steps (1 Peter 2:21).

This call to Christlikeness in suffering unjustly may well become increasingly relevant as persecution increases in many cultures today.

We are to be like Christ in his mission

Having looked at the teaching of Paul and Peter, we come now to the teaching of Jesus, as recorded by John (John 17:18; 20:21).

In prayer, Jesus said to his Father, 'As you sent me into the world, I have sent them into the world'; and in commissioning, he said, 'As the Father has sent me, I am sending you.' These words are immensely significant.

This is not just the version of the great commission recorded in John's Gospel, it is also an instruction that their mission in the world was to resemble Christ's. In what respect? The key words are 'sent into the world'. That is, as Christ had to enter our world, so we are to enter other people's worlds.

It was eloquently explained by Archbishop Michael Ramsay when he said:

> We state and commend the faith only in so far as we go out and put ourselves inside the doubts of the doubters, the questions of the questioners and the loneliness of those who have lost their way.[2]

This entering of other people's worlds is exactly what we mean by incarnational mission, and all authentic mission is incarnational mission. We are to be like Christ in his mission.

Here then are perhaps the five main ways in which we are to be Christlike: we are to be like Christ in his incarnation, in his service, in his love, in his endurance, and in his mission.

THREE PRACTICAL CONSEQUENCES

We conclude now with three practical consequences of the basis and examples for Christlikeness that we have considered.

Christlikeness and the mystery of suffering

Of course suffering is a huge subject in itself, and there are many ways in which Christians try to understand it. But one stands out, and that is that suffering is part of God's process of making us like Christ. Whether it is a disappointment or a frustration, we need to try to see it in the light of Romans 8:28 and 29.

According to Romans 8:28, God is always working for the good purpose of his people, and according to Romans 8:29 this good purpose is to make us like Christ.

Christlikeness and the challenge of evangelism

Why is it that our evangelistic efforts are often fraught with failure? Several reasons may be given, and I must not over-simplify, but one main reason is that we don't look like the Christ we proclaim.

'If you Christians lived like Jesus Christ, India would be at your feet tomorrow.'

John Poulton has written about this in his perceptive little book, *A Today Sort of Evangelism*:

The most effective preaching comes from those who embody the things they are saying. They *are* their message . . . Christians . . . need to look like what they are talking about. It is *people* who communicate primarily, not words or ideas . . . Authenticity . . . gets across from deep down inside people . . . A momentary insincerity can cast doubt on all that has made for communication up to that point . . . What communicates now is basically personal authenticity.[3]

Similarly, a Hindu professor, identifying one of his students as a Christian, once said, 'If you Christians lived like Jesus Christ, India would be at your feet tomorrow.'

Another example is of the Rev. Iskandar Jadeed, a former Arab Muslim, who has said, 'If all Christians were Christians there would be no more Islam today.'

I don't know the authors of these sayings personally but I believe them to be genuine.

Christlikeness and the indwelling of the Spirit

I have spoken much about Christlikeness, but how is it possible for us? In our own strength, it is clearly not, but God has given us his Holy Spirit to enable us to fulfil his purpose.

William Temple used to illustrate the point from Shakespeare in this way:

It is no good giving me a play like Hamlet or King Lear, and telling me to write a play like that. Shakespeare could do it; I can't.

And it is no good showing me a life like the life of Jesus and telling me to live a life like that. Jesus could do it; I can't.

But if the genius of Shakespeare could come and live in me, then I could write plays like his.

And if the Spirit of Jesus could come and live in me, then I could live a life like his.

God's purpose is to make us like Christ, and God's way is to fill us with his Holy Spirit.

Chapter 3

MATURITY

When I was travelling in the 1990s in the interests of the Langham Partnership International, I would often ask an audience how they would summarize the Christian scene in the world today. I would receive a variety of answers. But when invited to give my own answer to the question, I would sum it up in just three words, namely 'growth without depth'.

There is no doubt of the phenomenal growth of the church in many parts of the world. The statistics of church growth are amazing. 'Explosion' is not too dramatic a word to describe it. For example, the church in China has grown at least one hundred fold since the middle of the twentieth century. More Christian believers now worship God every Sunday in China than in all the churches of Western Europe put together.

At the same time we should not indulge in triumphalism, for it is often growth without depth.

There is superficiality of discipleship everywhere, and church leaders bemoan this situation. A leader from South Asia wrote to me recently that although the church in his country is growing numerically, 'there is a huge problem with lack of godliness and integrity'. And similarly an African leader has written that although he is well aware of the rapid growth of the African church, 'this growth is largely numerical . . . the church is without a strong biblical or theological foundation of her own'.

More striking still is a statement made in April 2006 in Los Angeles by Mrs Cao Shengjie, at that time President of the China Christian Council:

> Some say the church is doing well when there is growth in numbers . . . and we want to see people added to the church every day. But we are not only looking for numbers, but for the increase in numbers to go in parallel with the confirmation of the faith of the church.

These three quotations from Majority World leaders are enough to show that 'growth without depth', or statistical growth with no corresponding developing discipleship, is not a judgment imposed by the rest of the world – it is the view of the leaders themselves.

More than that, this situation is serious because it is displeasing to God. We dare to say this because the apostles whose letters we find in the New Testament rebuke their readers for their immaturity and urge them to grow up. Consider for example Paul's critique of the Corinthian church:

> Brothers and sisters, I could not address you as spiritual but as worldly – mere infants in Christ. I gave you milk, not solid food, for you were not yet ready for it. Indeed, you are still not ready. You are still worldly. For since there is jealousy and quarrelling among you, are you not worldly? Are you not acting like mere human beings? (1 Corinthians 3:1–3).

But there is another passage from the pen of Paul in which he writes about maturity, and it is on these verses that I propose to focus in this chapter:

> We proclaim [Christ], admonishing and teaching everyone with all wisdom, so that we may present everyone fully mature (*teleios*) in Christ. To this end I strenuously contend with all the energy Christ so powerfully works in me (Colossians 1:28–29).

The Greek adjective *teleios* occurs nineteen times in the New Testament and whether it is translated 'perfect' or 'mature' depends mainly on its context. It rarely if ever means 'perfect' in an absolute sense. Instead the *teleios* (person) is contrasted with the child or infant (e.g. 1 Corinthians 13:10–11). It is in this sense ('mature') that I think it best to understand the meaning of *teleios*.

Now in order to grasp the full significance of any biblical text, it is often a good thing to put it in the witness box and ply it with probing questions. This is what I propose to do with Colossians 1:28–29.

The first and essential question to ask concerns the nature of maturity. What is Christian maturity? The fact is that maturity is rather hard to pin down. Most of us suffer from lingering immaturities. Even in the grown adult the little child is still hiding somewhere.

Besides, there are different types of maturity. There is physical maturity (having a healthy well-developed body), intellectual maturity (having a trained mind and a coherent world-view), moral maturity (referring to people who 'have trained themselves to distinguish good from evil', Hebrews 5:14), and emotional maturity (having a balanced personality, able to establish relationships and assume responsibilities). But above all, there is spiritual maturity. What is that? Well, the apostle calls it maturity 'in Christ', that is, having a mature relationship with Christ.

Paul's most common way of defining Christians is to say that they are men and women 'in Christ', meaning not inside Christ as when our clothes are in a wardrobe and when tools are inside a chest, but rather as the branches are 'in' the vine and our limbs are 'in' the body, that is, united to Christ. So then, to be 'in Christ' is to be personally, vitally, organically related to him. In this sense, to be mature is to have a mature relationship with Christ in which we worship, trust, love and obey him.

The next question to ask is how do Christians become mature? Our text gives us a plain answer. Consider the basic skeleton of verse 28: 'We proclaim Christ . . . so that we may present everyone mature in Christ.'

To be mature is to have a mature relationship with Christ in which we worship, trust, love and obey him.

It is only logical. If Christian maturity is maturity in our relationship to Christ, in which we worship, trust and obey him, then the clearer our vision of Christ, the more convinced we become that he is worthy of our commitment.

In the introduction to his book *Knowing God*,[1] Dr J. I. Packer writes that we are 'pygmy Christians because we have a pygmy God'. We could equally say that we are pygmy Christians because we have a pygmy Christ. The truth is that there are many Jesuses on offer in the world's religious supermarkets, and many of them are false Christs, distorted Christs, caricatures of the authentic Jesus.

In our own day, for example, we find Jesus the capitalist and Jesus the socialist in competition with each other. Then there is Jesus the ascetic versus Jesus the glutton. And of course there have been the famous musicals – Jesus the clown of *Godspell* and *Jesus Christ Superstar*. There have been many more. But they have all been defective, and not one of them deserves our worship and our service. Each is what Paul called 'another Jesus', a Jesus different from the Jesus the apostles proclaimed.

So if we want to develop truly Christian maturity, we need above all a fresh and true vision of Jesus Christ – not least in his absolute supremacy which Paul sets out in the earlier half of Colossians 1, from verse 15 to verse 20. It is one of the sublimest Christological passages in the whole New Testament. Here is a loose paraphrase:

> Jesus is the visible image of the invisible God (verse 15), so that whoever has seen him has seen the Father. He is also 'the firstborn over all creation'. Not that he was himself created, but that he has rights of the firstborn, so that he is the creation's 'lord and head' (verse 16). For through him the universe was created. All things were created through him as agent and for him as head. Their unity and coherence are found in him. Also (verse 18) he is the head of the body, the church. He is the beginning and the firstborn from the dead, so that in everything he might have the pre-eminence.

For God was pleased (verses 19–20) both to have all his fullness dwell in Christ and also to reconcile all things to himself through Christ, making peace through the blood of his cross.

This is how Paul proclaimed Christ as Lord – as Lord of creation (the one through whom all things were made) and as Lord of the church (the one through whom all things have been reconciled). Because of who he is (the image and fullness of God) and because of what he has done (the one who brought about creation and reconciliation), Jesus Christ has a double supremacy. He is head of the universe and head of the church. He is the lord of both creations.

This is the apostle's masterful portrait of Jesus Christ. Where should we be but on our faces before him? Away then with our petty, puny, pygmy Jesuses! Away with our Jesus clowns and pop stars! Away too with our political Messiahs and revolutionaries! For these are caricatures. If this is how we think of him, then no wonder our immaturities persist.

Where then shall we find the authentic Jesus? The answer is that he is to be found in the Bible – the book which could be described as the Father's portrait of the Son painted by the Holy Spirit. The Bible is full of Christ. As he himself said, the Scriptures 'testify about me' (John 5:39). Jerome, the early Church Father, wrote that 'ignorance of Scripture is ignorance of Christ'. Equally, we may say that knowledge of Scripture is knowledge of Christ.

*Nothing is more important for
mature Christian discipleship than
a fresh, clear, true vision of the
authentic Jesus.*

If only the blindfold could be taken away from our eyes! If only we could see Jesus in the fullness of who he is and what he has done! Why then surely we would see how worthy he is of our wholehearted allegiance, and faith, love and obedience would be drawn out from us and we would grow into maturity. Nothing is more important for mature Christian discipleship than a fresh, clear, true vision of the authentic Jesus.

Now that we have defined Christian maturity and thought about how disciples become mature, we are ready for a third question, namely to whom is this call to maturity directed? It cannot have escaped our notice that in this text Paul repeats the word 'everyone': 'We proclaim Christ, admonishing and teaching everyone with all wisdom, so that we may present everyone fully mature in Christ' (Colossians 1:28). The background to this threefold repetition is likely to be what is known as the 'Colossian heresy'. Scholars are still debating the exact form which it took, but almost certainly it was an embryonic Gnosticism which became full-grown only in the middle of the second century.

These early Gnostics seem to have taught that there were two classes or categories of Christian. On the one hand there were *hoi polloi*, the common herd, who were united by *pistis*, faith. On the other hand there were *hoi teleioi*, the élite, who had been initiated into *gnosis*, special knowledge. Paul was horrified by this Christian elitism and set himself firmly against it. In his proclamation of Christ he hijacked the Gnostics' word *teleios* and applied it to everybody. He warned and taught everybody, he claimed, so that he might present everybody *teleios* (mature) in Christ. Maturity in Christ is emphatically not open only to the special few; it is open to everybody. Nobody need fail to attain it.

It is an interesting question of interpretation whether (as we study a biblical text) we identify with its author or with its readers. Sometimes (as here) it is reasonable to do both. It is certainly right to sit down alongside the Colossian Christians as they receive this message from Paul, and let him address us. In this way we will listen attentively to the apostle, receive his admonition about growing into maturity, determine to take our Bible reading yet more seriously, and as we read Scripture, look for Christ in order to love, trust and obey him. For the discipleship principle is clear: the poorer our vision of Christ, the poorer our discipleship will be, whereas the richer our vision of Christ, the richer our discipleship will be.

But it is also legitimate to stand alongside the apostle Paul as he addresses the Colossian Christians, especially if we are in a position of Christian leadership. It's true that he was an apostle and we are not. So we do not have his authority. Nevertheless, we do have pastoral responsibilities comparable to his, whether we are ordained or lay leaders.

So we need to note Paul's pastoral goal. The popular image of Paul is of an evangelist, the pioneer missionary and church planter, whose goal was to win converts, set up a church and move on. But this is only one side of the picture. Here he portrays himself as a pastor and teacher. His great longing, he writes, is to go beyond evangelism to discipleship, and to present everybody mature in Christ. And because this is the goal on which he spent his energies, so should we! 'To this end I labour, struggling with all his energy, which so powerfully works in me' (Colossians 1:29, NIV). Both Greek verbs ('labour' and 'struggle') express metaphors which imply physical exertion. The first is used of the farm labourer, and the second of the competitor in the Greek Games. Both conjure up a vision of rippling muscles and pouring sweat.

It's true that Paul could strive only with Christ's energy. Yet even with that divine energy he still needed to toil and struggle, no doubt in prayer and study. There can be no higher goal of ministry. What a wonderful slogan this is for anybody called to leadership – longing to present everybody for whom we are in any way responsible mature in Christ.

Looking back we can see a double responsibility: maturity in Christ is the goal both for ourselves and for our ministry to others.

So then may God give us such a full, clear vision of Jesus Christ, first that we may grow into maturity ourselves, and secondly that, by our faithful proclamation of Christ in his fullness to others, we may present others mature as well.

Chapter 4

CREATION-CARE

In pinpointing what (in my view) are several neglected aspects of radical discipleship, we must not suppose that these are limited to the personal and individual spheres. We should also be concerned with the wider perspective of our duties to God and our neighbour, part of which is the topic of this chapter: the care of our created environment.

The Bible tells us that in creation God established for human beings three fundamental relationships: first to himself, for he made them in his own image; second to each other, for the human race was plural from the beginning; and third, to the good earth and its creatures over which he set them.

Moreover, all three relationships were skewed by the fall. Adam and Eve were banished from the presence of the Lord God in the garden, they blamed each other for what had happened, and the good earth was cursed on account of their disobedience.

It stands to reason therefore that God's plan of restoration includes not only our reconciliation to God and to each other, but in some way the liberation of the groaning creation as well. We can certainly affirm that one day there will be a new heaven and a new earth (e.g. 2 Peter 3:13; Revelation 21:1), for this is an essential part of our hope for the perfect future that awaits us at the end of time. But meanwhile the whole creation is groaning, experiencing the birth pains of the new creation (Romans 8:18–23). How much of the earth's ultimate destiny can be experienced now is a matter for debate. But we can surely say that just as our understanding of the final destiny of our resurrection bodies should affect how we think of and treat the bodies we have at present, so our knowledge of the new heaven and earth should affect and increase the respect with which we treat it now.

What then should be our attitude to the earth? The Bible points the way by making two fundamental affirmations: 'The earth is the LORD's (Psalm 24:1), and 'The earth he has given to the human race' (Psalm 115:16).

In May 1999 I was privileged to take part in a day conference in Nairobi on 'Christians and the Environment'. Sharing the platform with me were Dr Calvin De Witt of

Au Sable Institute Michigan, and Peter Harris of A Rocha International. Participants that day included both leaders in the Kenyan government and representatives of churches, mission organizations and NGOs. The meeting received wide publicity. It was evident that creation care is neither a selfish interest of the developed 'north', nor a minority enthusiasm peculiar to birdwatchers or flower-lovers, but an increasingly mainline Christian concern.

The assertions that 'the earth is the Lord's' and that 'the earth he has given to the human race' complement rather than contradict each other.

Soon afterwards an *Evangelical Declaration on the Care of Creation* was published (1999) and the following year a substantial commentary appeared, edited by R. J. Berry and entitled *The Care of Creation*.[1]

The assertions that 'the earth is the Lord's' and that 'the earth he has given to the human race' complement rather than contradict each other. For the earth belongs to God by creation and to us by delegation. This does not mean that he has handed it over to us in such a way as to give up his own rights over it, but rather that he has given us the responsibility to preserve and develop the earth on his behalf.

How then should we relate to the earth? If we remember its creation by God and its delegation to us, we will avoid two opposite extremes and instead develop a third and better relationship to nature.

First, we will avoid *the deification of nature*. This is the mistake of pantheists who identify the Creator with his creation, of animists who populate the natural world with spirits, and of the New Age's *Gaia* movement which attributes to nature its own self-contained, self-regulating and self-perpetuating mechanisms. But all such confusions are insulting to the Creator. The Christian realization that nature is creation not Creator was an indispensable prelude to the whole scientific enterprise and is essential to the development of the earth's resources today. We *respect* nature because God made it; we do not *reverence* nature as if it were God.

Secondly, we must avoid the opposite extreme, which is *the exploitation of nature*. This is not to treat nature obsequiously as if it were God, nor to behave towards it arrogantly as if we were God. Genesis 1 has been unjustly blamed for environmental irresponsibility. It is true that God commissioned the human race to 'rule over' the earth and to 'subdue' it (Genesis 1:26–28), and that these two Hebrew verbs are forceful. But it would be absurd to imagine that he who *created* the earth then handed it over to us to be *destroyed*. No, the dominion God has given us should be seen as a *responsible stewardship*, not a destructive domination.

The third and correct relationship between human beings and nature is that of *cooperation with God*. To be sure, we are ourselves a part of creation, just as dependent on the Creator as are all his creatures. But at the same time he has deliberately humbled himself to make a divine-human partnership necessary. He created the earth but then told us to subdue it. He planted the garden, but then put Adam in it 'to work it and take care of it' (Genesis 2:15). This is often called the cultural mandate. For what God has given us is *nature*, whereas what we do with it is *culture*. We are not only to conserve the environment but also to develop its resources for the common good.

It is a noble calling to cooperate with God for the fulfilment of his purposes, to transform the created order for the pleasure and profit of all. In this way our work is to be an expression of our worship since our care of the creation will reflect our love for the Creator.

Another thought: it is possible to overstate this emphasis on human work in the conservation and transformation of the environment. In his excellent exposition of the first three chapters of Genesis *In the Beginning*,[2] Henri Blocher argues that the climax of Genesis 1 is not the creation of human beings as workers but the institution of the Sabbath for human beings as worshippers. The end point is not our toil (subduing the earth) but the laying aside of our toil on the Sabbath day. For the Sabbath puts the importance of work into perspective. It protects us from a total absorption in our work as if it were to be the be-all and end-all of our existence. It is not. We human beings find our humanness not only in relation to the earth, which we are to transform, but in relation to God whom we are to worship; not only in relation to the creation, but especially in relation to the Creator. God intends our work to be an expression of our worship, and our care of the creation to reflect our love for the Creator. Only then, whatever we do, in word or deed, shall we be able to do it to the glory of God (1 Corinthians 10:31).

These and other biblical themes are opened up in both the *Declaration* and the commentary on it. They deserve our careful study.[3]

THE ECOLOGICAL CRISIS

It is against the background of this wholesome biblical teaching that we need now to confront the current ecological crisis. It has been explored in a variety of ways but every analysis is likely to include the following four ingredients.

First, there is *the accelerating world population growth*. According to the population division of the United Nations in approximate terms, calculations began in AD 1804, which is when the population of the world reached 1 billion.[4] By the beginning of the twenty-first century (i.e. today) it had reached a total of 6.8 billion, while by the middle of the century it is reckoned that it will have reached the incredible total of 9.5 billion.

Because it is difficult to remember statistics, a simple mnemonic may help:

Past	1804	1 billion
Present	2000	6.8 billion
Future	2050	9.5 billion

How will it be possible to feed so many people, especially when approximately one-fifth of them lack the basic necessities for survival?

Secondly, there is *the depletion of the earth's resources*. It was E. F. Shumacher who, in his popular book *Small is Beautiful*,[5] drew the world's attention to the difference between capital and income. For example, fossil fuels are capital, once they are consumed they cannot be replaced. The appalling processes called deforestation and desertification are examples of the same principle. Others are the degradation or pollution of the plankton of the oceans, the green surface of the earth, living species and the habitats on which they depend for clean air and water.

Thirdly, *waste disposal*. An increasing population brings an increasing problem because of how to dispose safely of the undesirable by-products of manufacturing, packaging and consumption. The average person in the UK throws out his or her body weight in rubbish every three months. In 1994 a UK report entitled *Sustainable Development: The*

UK Strategy recommended a fourfold 'hierarchy of waste management' in an effort to contain this growing problem.

Fourthly, *climate change*. Of all the global threats which face our planet, this is the most serious.

Ultraviolet radiation in the atmosphere protects us, and if the ozone is damaged it exposes us to skin cancers and upsets our immune system. So when in 1983 a huge hole in the ozone layer appeared over the Antarctic and its neighbouring countries, it aroused a great deal of public alarm.

A few years later a similar hole appeared over the northern hemisphere. And by then it was recognized that the ozone depletion was due to chlorofluorocarbons (CFCs), the chemicals used in air conditioners, refrigerators and propellants. The Montreal Protocol called on the nations to halve the emission of CFCs by 1997.

Climate change is a related problem. The warmth of the earth's surface (essential for our planet's survival) is maintained by a combination of radiation from the sun and the infrared radiation it emits into space. This is the so-called 'greenhouse effect'. The pollution of the atmosphere by 'greenhouse gases' (especially carbon dioxide) reduces the infra-red emission and increases the temperature of the earth's surface. This is the spectre of global warming which may have disastrous consequences on the configuration of the world's geography and weather patterns.[6]

Reflecting on these four environmental hazards, one cannot help but see that our whole planet is in jeopardy.

'Crisis' is not too dramatic a word to use. What would be an appropriate response? To begin with, we can be thankful that at last in 1992 the so-called 'Earth Summit' was held in Rio and made a commitment to 'global sustainable development'. Subsequent conferences have ensured that environmental questions have been kept before the leading nations of the world.

But alongside these official conferences several NGOs have arisen. I will mention only the two most prominent explicitly Christian organizations, namely **Tearfund** and **A Rocha**, both having recently celebrated a special anniversary (forty and twenty-five years respectively).

Tearfund, founded by George Hoffman, is committed to development in the broadest sense and works in close cooperation with 'partners' in the Majority World. The wonderful story of Tearfund has been documented by Mike Hollow in his book *A Future and a Hope*.[7]

A Rocha is different, being much smaller. It was founded in 1983 by Peter Harris, who has documented its growth in two books: *Under the Bright Wings* (the first ten years) and *Kingfisher's Fire* (bringing the story up to date).[8] Its steady development is remarkable, as it now works in eighteen countries, establishing field study centres on all continents.

It is all very well to give our support to Christian environmental NGOs, but what are our individual responsibilities? I leave Chris Wright to answer the question, What can the radical disciple do to care for the creation?

Chris dreams of a multitude of Christians who care about creation and take their environmental responsibility seriously:

> They choose sustainable forms of energy where possible. They switch off unneeded appliances. They buy food, goods and services as far as possible from companies with ethically sound environmental policies. They join conservation societies. They avoid over-consumption and unnecessary waste and recycle as much as possible.[9]

What can the radical disciple do to care for the creation?

Chris also wants to see a growing number of Christians who include the care of creation within their biblical understanding of mission:

> In the past, Christians have instinctively been concerned about great and urgent issues in every generation . . . These have included the evils of disease, ignorance, slavery, and many other forms of brutality and exploitation. Christians have taken up the cause of widows, orphans, refugees, prisoners, the insane, the hungry – and most recently have

swelled the numbers of those committed to 'making poverty history'.

I want to echo Chris Wright's eloquent conclusion:

> It seems quite inexplicable to me that there are some Christians who claim to love and worship God, to be disciples of Jesus, and yet have no concern for the earth that bears his stamp of ownership. They do not care about the abuse of the earth and indeed, by their wasteful and over-consumptive life-styles, they collude in it.
>
> 'God intends . . . our care of the creation to reflect our love for the Creator.'[10]

To the LORD your God belong the heavens, even the highest heavens, the earth and everything in it (Deuteronomy 10:14).

Chapter 5

SIMPLICITY

A fifth characteristic of radical disciples, I suggest, is simplicity, especially in relation to the whole question of money and possessions. We postponed from Chapter 1 the challenge of materialism.

In March 1980 an International Consultation on Simple Lifestyle took place in England. It made a little impact at the time but in my view has received insufficient attention either then or since. So, let me introduce you to someone who attended the Consultation and whose life was influenced by it.

A SIMPLE LIFE

Dan Lam was born and brought up in a Christian home in Hong Kong. His father died when he was a young boy. So his mother brought up the family alone. She was a good and godly woman. On Sundays she would give each of her children some money to put in the offering plate, although they were quite poor. But Dan would take his share, sneak out of church, rent a bicycle and ride all over Hong Kong. When the service was over he would show up and return home with the family. According to one of his former class-mates, he was 'a very bad kid'.

When he was a teenager he fell ill and became so sick that he nearly died. It was then that he decided that God meant him 'good, not harm', and so he committed his life to the Lord Jesus Christ. He never looked back. It was a 180-degree change for him, to the amazement and relief of his family!

When the time came for him to earn his own living, he was employed by Bechtel Corporation, a multi-national engaged in heavy engineering work. At different times they have been involved in the construction of airports and seaports, in hurricane relief, in building the 'Chunnel' (the channel tunnel linking England and France) and in 'BART' the San Francisco Bay Area Rapid Transit system. Dan was not of course personally involved in all these projects, but he rose to be a manager responsible for several hundred employees.

In 1976 the company transferred him and his family to Saudi Arabia and in 1978 to London. It was then that I first met Dan and his wife Grace, for they joined All Souls Church, Langham Place, of which I was Rector, and were members of the same fellowship group.

Dan had a great concern for the poor and needy and he was generous to his family and his church, although his personal lifestyle was frugal. But he was also beginning to feel the pressures of business. Then came the Consultation on Simple Lifestyle and the challenge it brought. Dan had always tithed his income but now, he said, he must simplify his lifestyle even further. On a visit to India he saw real poverty, and also noticed that too high a percentage of mission funds went on overheads. He resolved not to accumulate wealth but to give it away.

In 1981 he resigned from Bechtel. It was not that he felt unable to serve God in a multi-national corporation, for Jesus Christ is Lord of all life. It was rather that he felt a particular calling to the countries of South East Asia to which he himself belonged: Thailand, Laos and Cambodia, together with Myanmar and Mongolia. He understood and applied indigenous principles in mission. He believed strongly in teaching and training Asians to win Asians and to equip Asians for mission. He was motivated by the knowledge that a majority of the world's population lives in Asia. Further, it is far more economical and efficient for Asian nationals to win Asians since nationals have no problem with culture or language, food or travel restrictions.

Dan started the first Bible School in Mongolia, and the Bible School in Phnom Penh (Cambodia) was at first registered in his name, though it is now registered as Phnom Penh Bible School. One heard of this significant growth with expectation. But it was not to last.

Suddenly Dan's leadership was taken away. For on 22nd March 1994 he was involved in a fatal air crash. He was flying in a Russian airbus (Aeroflot flight 593 from Moscow to Hong Kong) when it collided with a Russian hillside and all seventy-five passengers and crew perished. The cause was traced to the son of one of the pilots playing with the controls in the cockpit.

Grace, Dan's widow, and their two young children (Wei Wei and Justin) were of course devastated. But the work of the Lord went on.

Providentially, Dan's elder sister, Winnie, was in a position to take over with her husband, Joseph. They had travelled to the mission fields in which Dan had laboured and knew personally the Asian leaders with whom Dan had cooperated. And Dan had set up two foundations – one launched with his own funds and private, and the other a public charity named 'Country Network'. Through these foundations the unique work he had pioneered could be carried on.

Dan's legacy will last in the Asian believers he touched, and all because of the simple lifestyle he had embraced. 'The Simple Lifestyle Seminar,' Grace wrote in a letter to me, 'changed all of us.'

So let me now turn to the Consultation on Simple Lifestyle itself, and set out the evangelical commitment to simple lifestyle which so influenced Dan. Here it is.

AN EVANGELICAL COMMITMENT TO SIMPLE LIFESTYLE

Introduction
'Life' and 'lifestyle' obviously belong together and cannot be separated. All Christians claim to have received a new life from Jesus Christ. What lifestyle, then, is appropriate for them? If the life is new, the lifestyle should be new also. But what are to be its characteristics? In particular, how is it to be distinguished from the lifestyle of those who make no Christian profession? And how should this lifestyle reflect the challenges of the contemporary world – its alienation both from God and from the earth's resources which he created for the enjoyment of all?

*All Christians claim to have received
a new life from Jesus Christ.
What lifestyle, then, is appropriate
for them?*

It was such questions as these which led the participants in the Lausanne Congress on World Evangelization
(1974) to include in paragraph 9 of their Covenant these
sentences:

> All of us are shocked by the poverty of millions and disturbed
> by the injustices which cause it. Those of us who live in
> affluent circumstances accept our duty to develop a simple
> lifestyle in order to contribute more generously to both relief
> and evangelism.

These expressions have been much debated, and it became
clear that their implications needed to be carefully examined.

So the Theology and Education Group of the Lausanne
Committee for World Evangelization and the Unit on
Ethics and Society of the World Evangelical Fellowship's
Theological Commission agreed to co-sponsor a two-year
process of study, culminating in an international gathering.
Local groups met in fifteen countries. Regional conferences
were arranged in India, Ireland and the United States.
Then in March 1980, at High Leigh Conference Centre
near London, England, the international consultation
was convened. It brought together eighty-five evangelical
leaders from twenty-seven countries.

Our purpose was to study simple living in relation to
evangelism, relief and justice, since all three are mentioned
in the Lausanne Covenant's sentences on simple lifestyle.
Our perspective was on the one hand the teaching of

the Bible, and on the other the suffering world, that is, the billions of men, women and children who, though made in his image and the objects of his love, are either unevangelized or oppressed or both, being destitute of the gospel of salvation and of the basic necessities of human life.

During the four days of the consultation, we lived, worshipped, prayed and studied the Scriptures together; we listened to background papers (later published in a book) and heard some moving testimonies. We struggled to relate the theological and economic issues to one another which we debated both in plenary sessions and small groups. We laughed and cried and repented and made resolutions. Although at the beginning we sensed some tensions between representatives of the West and Majority Worlds, yet by the end the Holy Spirit of unity had brought us into a new solidarity of mutual respect and love.

Above all we tried to expose ourselves with honesty to the challenges of both the word of God and the world of need, in order to discern God's will and seek his grace to do it. In this process our minds were stretched, our consciences pricked, our hearts stirred and our wills strengthened.

We recognize that others have been discussing this topic for several years and we are ashamed that we have lagged behind them. We have no wish therefore to claim too much for our Consultation or commitment. Nor have we any grounds for boasting. Yet for us the week was historic and transforming. So we send this statement on its way for the study of individuals, groups and churches, with the earnest hope and prayer that large numbers of Christians will be moved, as we have been, to resolve, commitment and action.

John Stott	Ron Sider
Chairman	Convenor
Theology and Education	Unit on Ethics and Society
Working Group	Theological Commission of
Lausanne Committee for	the World Evangelical
World Evangelization	Fellowship

October, 1980

Preamble

For four days we have been together to consider the resolve expressed in the Lausanne Covenant (1974) to 'develop a simple lifestyle'. We have tried to listen to the voice of God through the pages of the Bible, through the cries of the hungry poor, and through each other. And we believe that God has spoken to us.

We thank God for his great salvation through Jesus Christ, for his revelation in Scripture which is a light for our path, and for the Holy Spirit's power to make us witnesses and servants in the world.

We are disturbed by the injustices of the world, concerned for its victims, and moved to repentance for our complicity in it. We have also been stirred to fresh resolves, which we have expressed in this commitment.

1. Creation

We worship God as the Creator of all things, and we celebrate the goodness of his creation. In his generosity he has given us everything to enjoy, and we receive it from his hands with humble thanksgiving (1 Timothy 4:4; 6:17). God's creation is marked by rich abundance and diversity, and he intends its resources to be husbanded and shared for the benefit of all.

We therefore denounce environmental destruction, wastefulness and hoarding. We deplore the misery of the poor who suffer as a result of these evils. We also disagree with the drabness of the ascetic. For all these deny the Creator's goodness and reflect the tragedy of the fall. We recognize our own involvement in them and we repent.

2. Stewardship

When God made man, male and female, in his own image, he gave them dominion over the earth (Genesis 1:26–28). He made them stewards of its resources, and they became responsible to him as Creator, to the earth which they were to develop, and to their fellow human beings with whom they were to share its riches. So fundamental are these truths that authentic human fulfilment depends on a right relationship to God, neighbour and the earth with all its resources. People's humanity is diminished if they have no just share in those resources.

By unfaithful stewardship, in which we fail to conserve the earth's finite resources, to develop them fully, or to distribute them justly, we both disobey God and alienate people from his purpose for them. We are determined therefore to honour God as the owner of all things, to remember that we are stewards and not proprietors of any land or property that we may have, to use them in the service of others, and to seek justice with the poor who are exploited and powerless to defend themselves.

We look forward to 'the restoration of all things' at Christ's return (Acts 3:21). At that time our full humanness will be restored, so we must promote human dignity today.

3. Poverty and wealth

We affirm that involuntary poverty is an offence against the goodness of God. It is related in the Bible to powerlessness, for the poor cannot protect themselves. God's call to rulers is to use their power to defend the poor, not to exploit them. The church must stand with God and the poor against injustice, suffer with them, and call on rulers to fulfil their God-appointed role.

We have struggled to open our minds and hearts to the uncomfortable words of Jesus about wealth. 'Be on your guard against all kinds of greed,' he said, and 'life does not consist in an abundance of possessions' (Luke 12:15). We have listened to his warnings about the dangers of riches.

For wealth brings worry, vanity and false security, the oppression of the weak and indifference to the sufferings of the needy. So it is hard for a rich person to enter the kingdom of heaven (Matthew 19:23), and the greedy will be excluded from it. The kingdom is a free gift offered to all, but it is especially good news for the poor because they benefit most from the changes it brings.

We believe that Jesus still calls some people (perhaps even us) to follow him in a lifestyle of total, voluntary poverty. He calls all his followers to an inner freedom from the seduction of riches (for it is impossible to serve God and money) and to sacrificial generosity ('to be rich in good works, to be generous and ready to share', 1 Timothy 6:18). Indeed, the motivation and model for Christian generosity are nothing less than the example of Jesus Christ himself who, though rich, became poor that through his poverty we might become rich (2 Corinthians 8:9). It was a costly, purposeful self-sacrifice; we mean to seek his grace to follow him. We resolve to get to know poor and oppressed people, to learn issues of injustice from them, to seek to relieve their suffering, and to include them regularly in our prayers.

4. The new community
We rejoice that the church is the new community of the new age, whose members enjoy a new life and a new lifestyle. The earliest Christian church, constituted in Jerusalem on the Day of Pentecost, was characterized by a quality of fellowship unknown before. Those Spirit-filled

believers loved one another to such an extent that they sold
and shared their possessions. Although their selling and
giving were voluntary, and some private property was
retained (Acts 5:4), it was made subservient to the needs
of the community. 'None of them said that anything he
had was his own' (Acts 4:32). That is, they were free from
the selfish assertion of proprietary rights. And as a result
of their transformed economic relationships, 'there was not
a needy person among them' (Acts 4:34).

This principle of generous and sacrificial sharing,
expressed in holding ourselves and our goods available for
people in need, is an indispensable characteristic of every
Spirit-filled church. So those of us who are affluent, in any
part of the world, are determined to do more to relieve the
needs of less privileged believers. Otherwise we shall be
like those rich Christians in Corinth who ate and drank
too much while their poor brothers and sisters were left
hungry, and we shall deserve the stinging rebuke Paul gave
them for despising God's church and desecrating Christ's
body (1 Corinthians 11:20–27). Instead, we determine to
resemble them at a later stage when Paul urged them out
of their abundance to give to the impoverished Christians
of Judea 'that there may be equality' (2 Corinthians
8:10–15). It was a beautiful demonstration of caring love
and of Gentile-Jewish solidarity in Christ.

In this same spirit we must seek ways to transact the
church's corporate business together with minimum
expenditure on travel, food and accommodation. We call

on churches and para-church agencies in their planning to be acutely aware of the need for integrity in corporate lifestyle and witness.

Christ calls us to be the world's salt and light, in order to hinder its social decay and illumine its darkness. But our light must shine and our salt must retain its saltness. It is when the new community is most obviously distinct from the world – in its values, standards and lifestyle – that it presents the world with a radically attractive alternative and so exercises its greatest influence for Christ. We commit ourselves to pray and work for the renewal of our churches.

5. Personal lifestyle

Jesus our Lord summons us to holiness, humility, simplicity and contentment. He also promises us his rest. We confess however that we have often allowed unholy desires to disturb our inner tranquillity. So without the constant renewal of Christ's peace in our hearts, our emphasis on simple living will be one-sided.

Our Christian obedience demands a simple lifestyle, irrespective of the needs of others. Nevertheless, the fact that 800 million people are destitute and that about 10,000 die of starvation every day make any other lifestyle indefensible.

While some of us have been called to live among the poor, and others to open our homes to the needy, all of us are determined to develop a simpler lifestyle. We intend to re-examine our income and expenditure, in order to manage on less and give away more. We lay down no rules or regulations for either ourselves or others. Yet we resolve to renounce waste and oppose extravagance in personal living, clothing and housing, travel and church building. We also accept the distinction between necessities and luxuries, creative hobbies and empty status symbols, modesty and vanity, occasional celebrations and normal routine, between service of God and slavery to fashion. Where to draw the line requires conscientious thought and decision by us, together with members of our families. Those of us who belong to the West need the help of our Majority World brothers and sisters in evaluating our standards of spending. Those of us who live in the Majority World acknowledge that we too are exposed to the temptation to covetousness. So we need one another's understanding, encouragement and prayers.

6. International development

We echo the words of the Lausanne Covenant: 'We are shocked by the poverty of millions, and disturbed by the injustices which cause it.' One quarter of the world's population enjoys unparalleled prosperity while another quarter endures grinding poverty. This gross disparity is an intolerable injustice; we refuse to acquiesce in it. The call for a new international economic order expresses the justified frustration of the Majority World.

We have come to understand more clearly the connection between resources, income and consumption: people often starve because they cannot afford to buy food, because they have no income, because they have no opportunity to produce, and because they have no access to power. We therefore applaud the growing emphasis of Christian agencies on development rather than aid. For the transfer of personnel and appropriate technology can enable people to make good use of their own resources while at the same time respecting their dignity. We resolve to contribute more generously to human development projects. Where people's lives are at stake, there should never be a shortage of funds.

But the action of governments is essential. Those of us who live in the affluent nations are ashamed that our governments have mostly failed to meet their targets for official development assistance, to maintain emergency food stocks or to liberalize their trade policy.

We have come to believe that in many cases multi-national corporations reduce local initiative in the countries where they work, and tend to oppose any fundamental change in government. We are convinced that they should become more subject to controls and more accountable.

7. Justice and politics
We are also convinced that the present situation of social injustice is so abhorrent to God that a large measure of change is necessary. Not that we believe in an earthly utopia. But neither are we pessimists. Change can come, although not through commitment to simple lifestyle or human development projects alone.

Poverty and excessive wealth, militarism and the arms industry, and the unjust distribution of capital, land and resources are issues of power and powerlessness. Without a shift of power through structural change these problems cannot be solved.

The Christian church, along with the rest of society, is inevitably involved in politics, which is 'the art of living in community'. Servants of Christ must express his lordship in their political, social and economic commitments and their love for their neighbours by taking part in the political process. How then can we contribute to change?

First, we will pray for peace and justice, as God commands. Secondly, we will seek to educate Christian people in the moral and political issues involved, and so clarify their vision and raise their expectations. Thirdly, we will take action. Some Christians are called to special tasks in government, economics or development. All Christians must participate in the active struggle to create a just and responsible society. In some situations obedience to God demands resistance to an unjust established order. Fourthly, we must be ready to suffer. As followers of Jesus, the Suffering Servant, we know that service always involves suffering.

While personal commitment to change our lifestyle without political action to change systems of injustice lacks effectiveness, political action without personal commitment lacks integrity.

8. Evangelism

We are deeply concerned for the vast millions of unevangelized people in the world. Nothing that has been said about lifestyle or justice diminishes the urgency of developing evangelistic strategies appropriate to different cultural environments. We must not cease to proclaim Christ as Saviour and Lord throughout the world. The church is not yet taking seriously its commission to be his witnesses 'to the ends of the earth' (Acts 1:8).

When Christians care for each other and for the deprived, Jesus Christ becomes more visibly attractive.

So the call to a responsible lifestyle must not be divorced from the call to responsible witness. For the credibility of our message is seriously diminished whenever we contradict it by our lives. It is impossible with integrity to proclaim Christ's salvation if he has evidently not saved us from greed, or his lordship if we are not good stewards of our possessions, or his love if we close our hearts against the needy. When Christians care for each other and for the deprived, Jesus Christ becomes more visibly attractive.

In contrast to this, the affluent lifestyle of some Western evangelists when they visit the Majority World is understandably offensive to many.

We believe that simple living by Christians generally would release considerable resources, finance and personnel for evangelism as well as for development. So by our commitment to a simple lifestyle we recommit ourselves wholeheartedly to world evangelization.

9. The Lord's return

The Old Testament prophets both denounced the idolatries and injustices of God's people and warned of his coming judgment. Similar denunciations and warnings are found in the New Testament. The Lord Jesus is coming back soon to judge, to save and to reign. His judgment will fall upon the greedy (who are idolaters) and upon all oppressors. For on that day the King will sit upon his throne and separate the saved from the lost. Those who have ministered to him by ministering to one of the least of his needy brothers and sisters will be saved, for the reality of saving faith is exhibited in serving love. But those who are persistently indifferent to the plight of the needy, and so to Christ in them, will be irretrievably lost (Matthew 25:31–46). All of us need to hear again this solemn warning of Jesus, and resolve afresh to serve him in the deprived. We therefore call on our fellow Christians everywhere to do the same.

Our resolve

So then, having been freed by the sacrifice of our Lord Jesus Christ, in obedience to his call, in heartfelt compassion for the poor, in concern for evangelism, development and justice, and in solemn anticipation of the day of judgment, we humbly commit ourselves to develop a just and simple lifestyle, to support one another in it, and to encourage others to join us in this commitment.

We know that we shall need time to work out its implications and that the task will not be easy. May Almighty God give us grace to be faithful! Amen.

* * * *

The *Evangelical Commitment to Simple Lifestyle* is a lengthy document. So let me highlight its essential emphases:

1. **The new community:** we rejoice that the church is intended to be God's new community, which exhibits new values, new standards and a new lifestyle.
2. **Personal lifestyle:** we lay down no rules or regulations, but in view of the fact that about 10,000 people die of starvation every day, we determine to simplify our lifestyle.
3. **International development:** we are shocked by the poverty of millions and resolve to contribute more generously to human development projects. But government action is essential.

4. **Justice and politics:** we believe that the present situation of social injustice is abhorrent to God and that change can and must come.

5. **Evangelism:** we are deeply concerned for the vast millions of unevangelized peoples. The call to a simple lifestyle must not be divorced from the call to responsible witness.

6. **The Lord's Return:** we believe that when Jesus returns, those who have ministered to him by ministering to the least will be saved, for the reality of saving faith is exhibited in serving love.

Chapter 6

BALANCE

The late Duke of Windsor, who had for a short period been King Edward VIII, died in Paris in May 1972. That night a very interesting documentary was shown on British television. It included extracts from earlier films in which he was shown being questioned about his upbringing, his brief reign and his abdication.

Looking back to his boyhood he said, 'My father [King George V] was a strict disciplinarian. Sometimes when I had done something wrong, he would admonish me saying "My dear boy, you must always remember who you are".' If only he would remember that he was a royal prince destined for the throne, he would behave accordingly and not misbehave.

So who are we? That is the question. I doubt if there is any New Testament text which gives a more varied and balanced account of what it means to be a disciple than 1 Peter 2:1–17:

Therefore, rid yourselves of all malice and all deceit, hypocrisy, envy, and slander of every kind. Like newborn babies, crave pure spiritual milk, so that by it you may grow up in your salvation, now that you have tasted that the Lord is good.

As you come to him, the living Stone – rejected by human beings but chosen by God and precious to him – you also, like living stones, are being built into a spiritual house to be a holy priesthood, offering spiritual sacrifices acceptable to God through Jesus Christ. For in Scripture it says:

'See, I lay a stone in Zion,
    a chosen and precious cornerstone,
and the one who trusts in him
    will never be put to shame.'

Now to you who believe, this stone is precious. But to those who do not believe,

'The stone the builders rejected
    has become the cornerstone,'

and,

'A stone that causes people to stumble
and a rock that makes them fall.'

They stumble because they disobey the message – which is also what they were destined for.

But you are a chosen people, a royal priesthood, a holy nation, God's special possession, that you may declare the praises of him who called you out of darkness into his wonderful light. Once you were not a people, but now you are the people of God; once you had not received mercy, but now you have received mercy.

Dear friends, I urge you, as foreigners and exiles, to abstain from sinful desires, which war against your soul. Live such good lives among the pagans that, though they accuse you of doing wrong, they may see your good deeds and glorify God on the day he visits us.

Submit yourselves for the Lord's sake to every human authority: whether to the emperor, as the supreme authority, or to governors, who are sent by him to punish those who do wrong, and to commend those who do right. For it is God's will that by doing good you should silence the ignorant talk of the foolish. Live as free people, but do not use your freedom as a cover-up for evil; live as God's slaves. Show proper respect to everyone: Love your fellow-believers, fear God, honour the emperor.

In a series of varied metaphors the apostle illustrates who we are. Each carries with it a corresponding obligation.

Together they might be called Christianity according to Peter.

BABIES

The reason why Peter likens his readers to *newborn babies* is that they have been born again (1 Peter 1:23). What, then, is the new birth? It is a mistake to identify this with what happens when we are baptized as members of the church. To be sure, baptism is the sacrament of the new birth. That is, it is the outward and visible dramatization of it. But we must not confuse the symbol with the reality, or the sign with the thing signified.

No, the new birth is a deep, inward, radical change, brought about by the Holy Spirit in our human personality by which we receive a new heart and a new life and become a new creation. Furthermore, as Jesus insisted in his conversation with Nicodemus, it is indispensable. 'You must be born again,' he said (John 3:7).

The point is that we do not emerge from the new birth with the understanding and character of a mature Christian, still less with the fully grown wings of an angel (!) but rather 'like newborn babies' – weak, immature, vulnerable and needing above all to grow. This is why the New Testament speaks of our need to grow in knowledge, holiness, faith, love and hope. So Peter writes here that his readers must 'grow up' in their salvation (verse 2). The matching truth is that they are to rid themselves of 'all malice and all deceit, hypocrisy, envy and slander of every kind' (verse 1), for (he

implies) these things are babyish. So we are to grow out of
them and grow into Christlikeness.

But how are we to grow? Staying with the picture of
newborn babies, we note Peter's reference in verse 2 to 'pure
spiritual milk': 'Like newborn babies, crave pure spiritual
milk, so that by it you may grow up in your salvation.'

In other words, just as the secret of the healthy growth
of a child is the regularity of a right diet, so daily disciplined
feeding is the major condition of spiritual growth.

What then is the milk which we are to consume if we
are to grow into Christian maturity? According to the TNIV
it is 'pure spiritual milk'. The Greek adjective is *logikos*.
This could mean 'metaphysical' as opposed to literal
cow's milk, or 'rational' meaning food for the mind as for
the body, or 'the milk of the word', as in 1:23. Certainly
God's word is as indispensable to our spiritual growth as
maternal milk is to a baby's growth. 'Crave it,' Peter urges,
'now that you have tasted that the Lord is good' (verse 3).
E. G. Selwyn in his commentary[1] suggests that Peter has
in mind 'the ardour of a suckled child'. You have had a
taste, Peter seems to be saying, now get a thirst.

There is a great need for daily discipline in the Christian
life. William Temple, Archbishop of Canterbury during
the Second World War, said to a large crowd of young
people:

> The loyalty of Christian youth must be first and foremost to
> Christ himself. Nothing can take the place of the daily time

of intimate companionship with the Lord . . . make time for
it somehow and secure that it is real.

STONES

The second picture which Peter develops is that of *living
stones* (verses 4–8). He turns from the world of biology
(birth and growth) to the world of architecture (stones and
buildings). We have been in a maternity ward watching a
new baby thirsting for its milk; we now move outside and
watch a building under construction. It is a stone building
and we have no difficulty recognizing it as a church –
not the sort of church building we know today but the
church of the living God, the people of God. Since the
stones in the building are people, Peter calls them 'living
stones'.

Let's pause a moment and rejoice that all over the world
God is building his church. Other faiths (ancient and
modern) may experience a resurgence, secularism may
make inroads into the church of the West, and hostile
groups and governments may persecute the church and
drive it underground. But the church continues to grow.

In fact nothing can destroy God's church. Jesus promised
that the 'gates of death will not overcome it' (Matthew
16:18). That is, the church has an eternal destiny. It is
indestructible. Stone by stone the building grows until
one day the coping stone will be put in place and the
construction is complete.

How then do we join the church? We join the visible, outward expression of the church by baptism. But how do we become members of the people of God? See verse 4: 'Come to him', to that living Stone, i.e. Jesus Christ, 'rejected by human beings' but in God's sight 'precious' and be built into a spiritual house. In verses 6–8 Peter gathers together a series of Old Testament texts (from Jeremiah and the Psalms) on the subject of rocks and stones. It is significant that he then applies them to Christ and not to himself. For Peter is not the rock on which we are to build our lives: Christ is the Living Stone rejected by Israel but chosen by God and precious to him.

What is the implication of all this? It is surely that we belong to one another. If babies need milk in order to grow, stones need mortar in order to stick to one another. Look in your imagination at the building. Each stone is cemented in with other stones and so is part of the building. No stone is suspended in mid-air. Every stone belongs to the building and cannot be dislodged from it.

Let's pause a moment and reflect, applying Peter's teaching to ourselves. What does Jesus Christ mean to us? Is he a stumbling-stone against whom we scrape our shins and fall? Or is he the foundation stone on which we are building our lives?

Some years ago I had the opportunity of meeting and speaking with Dr Hobart Mowrer,[2] Emeritus Professor of Psychiatry at the University of Illinois. He was well known in his day. He was not a Christian, he told me, and had

had a lover's quarrel with the church. Why? Because, he said, the church had failed him as a young man and continued to fail his patients today. And he added: 'The church has never learned the secret of community.' This was his answer. It is one of the most damning criticisms of the church I have ever heard. For the church *is* community, living stones in the building of God.

We need to recapture a vision of the church as fellowship, as living stones in the building of God. Moreover, there is a great need for better quality mortar.

PRIESTS

So far Peter has likened us to newborn babies with the duty to grow up, and to living stones with the duty to love and support one another. Now he comes to his third picture as he likens us to *holy priests* with the duty to worship God.

This metaphor comes as a surprise, even a shock, to many Christians. Yet we cannot avoid it. God has made us, Peter writes, both 'a holy priesthood' (verse 5) and 'a royal priesthood' (verse 9). What on earth did the apostle mean?

In Old Testament days the Israelite priests enjoyed two exclusive privileges. First they enjoyed access to God. Herod's temple was surrounded by the court of the priests, from which the lay people were rigorously excluded. Only the priests were allowed into the temple itself, while only the high priest could enter the holy of holies or inner sanctuary, and then only on the day of atonement. To underline this, the law prescribed the death penalty to all intruders. This symbolized that access to God was restricted to the priesthood and denied to the lay people.

The second privilege enjoyed by the priests was the offering of sacrifices to God. The lay people brought their sacrifices and laid their hands on the head of their victim, both to identify themselves with it and symbolically to transfer their guilt to it. But only the priests were allowed to kill the sacrifices, to perform the ritual and sprinkle the blood.

In Old Testament times then, access and sacrifice were the two privileges which were strictly reserved for the priesthood.

But now in and through Jesus Christ this distinction between priest and people has been abolished. The privileges which were previously limited to the priests are now shared by all, for all are priests. The whole church is a priesthood. Through Christ all of us enjoy access to God (we have boldness to enter into the holy presence of God, Hebrews 10:19–22). Through Christ all of us offer to God the spiritual sacrifices of our worship. This is 'the priesthood of all believers' which the Reformers recovered at the Reformation.

Of course some Christians are still called to be pastors, and in the Anglican church some pastors are called 'priests'. This is not because we have forgotten our Reformation heritage and claim a priestly role denied the laity. It is rather because the English word 'priest' (as any dictionary will tell us) is a contraction of the word 'presbyter' meaning 'elder' and has no priestly connotation. This is why Anglicans in the seventeenth century retained the word 'priest' in the Book of Common Prayer. But it can be confusing and I admire the wisdom of the leaders of the Church of South India and the Church of Pakistan in naming their three orders of ministry 'bishops, presbyters and deacons'.

Why then are Christian disciples called 'a holy priesthood'? Peter tells us in verse 5:

> You are being built into a spiritual house to be a holy priesthood, offering spiritual sacrifices acceptable to God through Jesus Christ.

Thus we are holy priests called to worship God. But is that all? Is the church to be a kind of spiritual ghetto? Are we engrossed in our own interior life? Are our only activities personal growth (as babies), fellowship (like stones in a building) and worship (offering God the spiritual sacrifices of our praise)? What about the lost and lonely world outside? Don't we care about it?

GOD'S PEOPLE

These questions lead us to verses 9 and 10 in which Peter develops a fourth metaphor: 'But you are a chosen people, a royal priesthood, a holy nation, God's special possession.'

Here the apostle likens the church to a nation or people, in fact, to *God's own people* or possession. What is fascinating about these expressions is where Peter got them from. He did not invent them but found them in Exodus 19:5–6, where God said to Israel newly redeemed from Egypt that if they kept his covenant by obeying his commandments, they would be his treasured possession (*sĕgullâ*), his nation out of all the nations of the earth, a holy nation.

Here in this letter, with great audacity given him by the Holy Spirit, Peter lifts these words out of Exodus where they applied to Israel and reapplies them to the Christian community. You followers of Jesus, he is saying to us today, are what Israel used to be – 'a holy nation', though now an international one.

But why did God choose Israel? And why has he chosen us?

The answer is not out of favouritism, but in order to be his *witnesses*; not that we might enjoy a monopoly of the gospel, but that we might declare 'the praises (or 'excellencies' or 'mighty deeds') of him who called you out of darkness into his wonderful light'.

For at one time, Peter continues, quoting from the book of Hosea:

you were not a people, but now you are God's people;
you had not received mercy, but now you have received
    mercy;

you were in darkness, but now you are in his wonderful
    light.

Now then, we cannot possibly keep these blessings to
ourselves!

FOREIGNERS

So far Peter has likened us –

- to newborn babies, with the responsibility of growth
- to living stones, with the responsibility of fellowship
- to holy priests, with the responsibility of worship
- to God's own people, with the responsibility of witness.

Peter still has two more pictures, and with verse 11 he
introduces his fifth: 'Dear friends, I urge you, as *foreigners
and exiles*, to abstain from sinful desires, which war against
your soul.' The Greek words are interesting. The word for
'foreigners' indicates people who have no rights where they
live, while 'exiles' are those who have no home.

Why did Peter describe his readers by these words? Partly
because this is what they were literally. They were scattered
throughout the Roman Empire. They belonged to what
was known as the 'diaspora' (1:1), in particular throughout the five provinces of Pontus, Galatia, Cappadocia,
Asia and Bithynia (modern Turkey). But in addition this
symbolized their spiritual condition. Now that they had

been born again into the kingdom of God, they had
become to some degree 'foreigners and exiles on earth'.
Therefore they were now citizens of two countries. And
because their primary citizenship was heavenly, they were
called to holiness.

This concept of a holy and heavenly 'citizenship' is
a dangerous truth, for it can easily be distorted. Indeed
it often has been misused and become an excuse to opt
out of our earthly responsibilities. Karl Marx has not
always been mistaken in his assertion that religion is 'the
opium of the people' – drugging them to acquiesce in
the injustices of the status quo while promising them
justice in the world to come.

But Peter is careful to avoid this travesty of the truth.
For he moves straight from his reference to our pilgrim
status to our citizenship duties on earth. More of this
anon.

SERVANTS

Peter's sixth picture shows disciples as *conscientious servants
of God* (verses 12–17). Peter urges his readers to live such
good lives among the pagans that they may see their good
deeds, to submit to the secular authorities, to do good and
so silence the ignorant talk of the foolish; to live as free
people without misusing their freedom; but to live as
God's slaves and to show proper respect to everyone: fellow-
believers, God and the authorities.

Nevertheless, in spite of all these earthly duties as conscientious citizens,
    submitting to authorities
        silencing criticism
            doing good
                respecting everybody

- We still belong first to heaven!
- We are aliens and exiles on earth.
- We are pilgrims travelling home to God.

This fact (our heavenly citizenship) profoundly challenges our attitudes: to money and possessions, as we see life as a pilgrimage between two moments of nakedness; to tragedy and suffering, as we see them in the perspective of eternity; and especially our attitude to temptation and sin.

Verse 11 draws a deliberate contrast between 'sinful desires' and 'soul'. Our soul is on its way to God. So we should abstain from everything which might hinder its progress, and must live a holy life in preparation for the holy presence of God in heaven.

BALANCE

My readers may well have been wondering why I have entitled this chapter with the one word 'Balance'. The reason should now become clear. We have followed Peter in the six metaphors which go to make up the portrait he paints of the disciple. Here they are again:

- as newborn babies we are called to growth,
- as living stones to fellowship,
- as holy priests to worship,
- as God's own people to witness,
- as aliens and strangers to holiness,
- as servants of God to citizenship.

This is a beautifully comprehensive and balanced portrait. These six duties seem to resolve themselves into three couplets, each of which contains a balance.

We are called to both individual discipleship and corporate fellowship . . . worship and work . . . and pilgrimage and citizenship.

First, we are called to both individual discipleship and corporate fellowship. Babies, although born into a family, have their own identity. Even twins are born one by one! But the primary function of the stones used in building is to be part of something else. They have surrendered their individuality to the building. Their significance is not in themselves but in the whole. So we need to emphasize both our individual and our corporate responsibilities.

Secondly, we are called to both worship and work. As a priesthood we worship God. As God's own people we witness to the world. The church is a worshipping, witnessing community.

Thirdly, we are called to both pilgrimage and citizenship.

In each couplet we are called to balance, and not to emphasize either at the expense of the other. Thus we are both individual disciples and church members, both worshippers and witnesses, both pilgrims and citizens.

Nearly all our failures stem from the ease with which we forget our comprehensive identity as disciples. Our Heavenly Father is constantly saying to us what King George V kept saying to the Prince of Wales, 'My dear child, you must always remember who you are, for if you remember your identity you would behave accordingly.'

Chapter 7

DEPENDENCE

So-called 'secular' theologians in the 1960s boldly asserted that humanity had come of age and that we can now dispense with God. Their shocking declaration was short-lived, however, for the truth is that we are sinners who are dependent on God for his mercy and for his continuing grace. To attempt to live without him is precisely what is meant by sin. We also need one another.

Let me share with you a recent experience of mine which demonstrated my weakness and dependence. It was Sunday morning, 20th August, 2006, and I was due to preach in All Souls Church, Langham Place, London. I was putting away some clean laundry when I tripped over the protruding feet of a swivel chair and fell between my bed and a bookcase. I knew at once that I had broken or dislocated my hip, for I could not move, let alone get up. I was able, however, to push the panic button I was wearing and kind friends immediately came to my rescue.

Hugh Palmer, rector of All Souls, found my sermon notes and somehow managed to preach my sermon. Only later did I note its appropriateness. For I had prepared an exposition of the Lord's Prayer.[1] It consists of six petitions: three expressing our passion for the glory of God (his name, kingdom and will), followed by three expressing our dependence on his grace (for our daily bread, forgiveness of our sins and deliverance from evil). It had long seemed to me that the second half of the Lord's Prayer is a summary of our discipleship – our concern for God's glory and our dependence on his mercy. Dependence is a fundamental attitude for all of us whenever we say the Lord's Prayer.

Even while the sermon on dependence was being preached, it was at least being partially illustrated. Within an amazingly short time I had been moved, inert, from floor to stretcher, from stretcher to ambulance, from ambulance to hospital bed, from hospital bed to operating theatre. I woke up to find myself gratefully supplied with a replacement hip, and in due course I have been rehabilitated.

So as this chapter progresses please do not forget my earlier experiences, spreadeagled on the floor, completely dependent on others. For this is where, from time to time, the radical disciple needs to be. I believe that the dependence involved in these experiences can be used by God to bring about greater maturity in us.

There is another aspect of the dependence which I experienced which was new to me, which I am tempted to gloss over, but which my trusted friends have urged me not to conceal. It is the emotional weakness which physical infirmity sometimes brings to the surface and which finds expression in weeping.

I am not naturally a weepy person, and am generally regarded as a strong and not a weak person, having been brought up at Rugby School, one of those so-called 'public' schools where one is supposed to be taught the philosophy of the stiff upper lip, that is, being discouraged from showing any emotion.

But then I read the Gospels and discovered that Jesus our Lord is recorded as having wept in public twice: once over the impenitent city of Jerusalem (Luke 19:41), and again at the graveside of Lazarus (John 11:35).

So, if Jesus wept, his disciples may presumably do so also.

But why should I have shed tears? I was faced with neither impenitence nor death. Was I wallowing in self-pity over my prospect of a slow return to health? Was I regretting my fall and fracture? Did I already glimpse the end of my public ministry? No, I really did not have time to collect my thoughts into order.

I had a similar experience of weeping with my friend John Wyatt, who is Professor of Ethics and Perinatology at University College Hospital in London, and has become well known for his defence of the sanctity of human life in public debates on abortion and euthanasia. When he visited me in hospital, we shared our experiences of weakness and dependence and we both broke down in tears. Here is how he describes it:

> In the first days following surgery John Stott was troubled by episodes of disorientation and by vivid and alarming visual hallucinations. In addition there were the inevitable indignities of receiving nursing care, and concerns about what the future would hold. As we talked and shared together in the hospital, I was strongly reminded of my own experience of severe illness and confusion some years previously. I remember we both found ourselves in tears, overcome by a powerful sense of our common human vulnerability and frailty. It was a painful but liberating experience.

And here is a second and similar experience, this time contributed by Sheila Moore, my friend and physiotherapist. She describes it as follows:

> Soon after arriving home following convalescence, John had just returned to rest in a chair, when he suddenly shuddered and sighed deeply. I looked up to see if he was unwell, and realized that tears were flowing freely. He was experiencing an overwhelming release of all the emotional build-up and challenge of recent events, which he had so patiently dealt with as 'a patient'.

There are no words to say during such a deep experience – just empathy and a comforting firm hand on his shoulder. As the emotion gradually subsided, I reassured him that this was not an uncommon experience in such circumstances, and that tears are a very valuable release and form of healing.

This completely 'out-of-character' experience happened suddenly, as a total surprise causing some shock and emotional pain. It can be difficult to rationalize such experiences, especially for men, who tend to view them as an indignity. But also if faced with honesty they can be a wonderful relief. It would be valuable to view these moments as a God-given preparation for the changes in life that lie ahead, and as a special gift from God.

Let me give you another illustration.

The man who led me to Christ during my last years at Rugby School was the Rev. E. J. H. Nash, known to all his many friends as 'Bash'. He was a man of outstanding Christian commitment who had a clear vision to win the boys of the top public schools for Christ. Through camps or house parties he was remarkably successful. Despite success in this ministry, he showed no signs of arrogance. On the contrary, everybody who met him commented on his humility, and many of us who were his friends were curious to discover its secret. He was very reticent to talk about it, but he did divulge it to me.

Bash and I were travelling together by train one day when he told me about his early life. When he was in his twenties he was struck by a serious illness. At its height he thought he was on his deathbed. He became so weak that he could hardly move. He could not even feed himself but had to be fed with a spoon. It was, he continued, an experience of total dependence and at the same time of humiliation. Indeed, humiliation, he concluded, was the road to humility. Having plumbed the depths of utter helplessness, it would be impossible to climb the hill of self-confidence.

Some years later this truth was confirmed by Michael Ramsey, Archbishop of Canterbury.

Humiliation, he concluded, was the road to humility. Having plumbed the depths of utter helplessness, it would be impossible to climb the hill of self-confidence.

Addressing a group of people on the eve of their ordination, on one occasion he chose humility as his topic, and his address included the following advice:

1. *Thank God*, often and always . . . Thank God, carefully and wonderingly for your continuing privileges . . . Thankfulness is a soil in which pride does not easily grow.

2. Take care about the *confession of your sins*. Be sure to criticise yourself in God's presence: that is your self-examination. Put yourself under the divine criticism: that is your confession . . .

3. Be ready to accept *humiliations*. They can hurt terribly, but they help you to be humble. There can be the trivial humiliations. Accept them. There can be the bigger humiliations . . . All these can be so many chances to be a little nearer to our humble and crucified Lord . . .

4. Do not worry about *status* . . . There is only one status that our Lord bids us to be concerned with, and that is the status of proximity to himself . . .

5. Use your *sense of humour*. Laugh about things, laugh at the absurdities of life, laugh about yourself, and about your own absurdity. We are all of us infinitesimally small and ludicrous creatures within God's universe. You have to be serious, but never be solemn, because if you are solemn about anything, there is the risk of becoming solemn about yourself.[2]

A refusal to be dependent on others is not a mark of maturity but immaturity. A good example is the film *Driving Miss Daisy* based on the Pulitzer Prize-winning play by Alfred Uhry.

Although there is an undercurrent of racial tension, the main plot is the developing psychological relationship between the two chief characters, namely Miss Daisy, the stubborn seventy-two-year-old widow and her African-American driver, Hoke.

The action begins when Miss Daisy crashes her car by putting her foot on the accelerator instead of the brake. Her son, Boolie, tells her that no insurance company will now insure her and that she must get a chauffeur. She refuses but he perseveres until he finds Hoke who has driven a local judge until he died.

In the beginning she will have nothing to do with Hoke. On one occasion she blurts out, 'I don't need you, I don't want you, I don't like you!' But gradually as Miss Daisy and Hoke spend time together, they grow to appreciate each other until years later she says to him, 'You're my best friend. Really', and takes his hand.

The film ends on a Thanksgiving Day in the retirement home where Miss Daisy now lives. Boolie and Hoke both visit her, but she insists on monopolizing Hoke. He notices that she has not eaten her pumpkin pie, and as she tries to pick up her fork, he gently takes the plate and fork from her. 'Lemme hep' you wid' it,' he says. He cuts a small piece of pie and carefully feeds it to her. She is delighted. It tastes good. He feeds her another. And another.

The film documents the transformation in their relationship from the early days when she refused to be dependent on him for anything, to the end when she is dependent on others for nearly everything.

Ageing is the process which changed the relationship between Miss Daisy and Hoke. By the time the film came to its end, Hoke was eighty-five years old and Miss Daisy ninety-seven.

And still today our relationships are subject to change. The late Dr Paul Tournier (1898–1986), the well-known Swiss physician and psychotherapist, made his name with his book *The Meaning of Persons*,[3] and applied his thinking to his book *Learning to Grow Old*:

> We are called to become more personal, to become persons, to face old age with all our personal resources.
>
> We have given things priority over persons, we have built a civilisation based on things rather than on persons. Old people are discounted because they are purely and simply persons, whose only value is as persons and not as producers any more.
>
> When we are old . . . , we have the time and the qualifications necessary to a true ministry of personal relationships.[4]

But we must not imagine that dependence is the only appropriate attitude to be adopted by a radical disciple. There are times and seasons in which we are called to the opposite, namely independence rather than dependence. In fact, Myra Chave-Jones, who was largely responsible in the 1960s for founding Care and Counsel, a Christian counselling service in London, has written that the struggle between dependence and independence 'is one of life's steepest learning curves'.

Jesus himself taught that dependence grows as we grow. After his resurrection he said to Peter:

When you were younger you dressed yourself and went where
you wanted; but when you are old you will stretch out your
hands, and someone else will dress you and lead you where
you do not want to go (John 21:18).

John tells us that Jesus' words had a specific reference to
Peter and his death, but they embody a principle of wider
application to growing old.

So, although independence is appropriate in some
circumstances, I come back to dependence as the most
characteristic attitude for the radical disciple. I turn to John
Wyatt (already mentioned) for an eloquent expression of
the priority of dependence: 'God's design for our life is that
we should be dependent.'

We come into this world totally dependent on the love,
care and protection of others. We go through a phase of
life when other people depend on us. And most of us will
go out of this world totally dependent on the love and care
of others. And this is not an evil, destructive reality. It is
part of the design, part of the physical nature which God
has given us.

I sometimes hear old people, including Christian people
who should know better, say 'I don't want to be a burden
to anyone else. I'm happy to carry on living so long as I can
look after myself, but as soon as I become a burden I would
rather die.' But this is wrong. We are all designed to be a
burden to others. You are designed to be a burden to me
and I am designed to be a burden to you. And the life of

the family, including the life of the local church family, should be one of 'mutual burdensomeness'. 'Carry each other's burdens, and in this way you will fulfil the law of Christ' (Galatians 6:2).

Christ himself takes on the dignity of dependence. He is born a baby, totally dependent on the care of his mother. He needs to be fed, he needs his bottom to be wiped, he needs to be propped up when he rolls over. And yet he never loses his divine dignity. And at the end, on the cross, he again becomes totally dependent, limbs pierced and stretched, unable to move. So in the person of Christ we learn that dependence does not, cannot, deprive a person of their dignity, of their supreme worth. And if dependence was appropriate for the God of the universe, it is certainly appropriate for us.

Chapter 8

DEATH

The eighth and last characteristic of the radical disciple which I have chosen is death. Let me explain. Christianity offers life – eternal life, life to the full. But it makes it plain that the road to life is death. It underlines this in at least six areas, as I will go on to show in this chapter. Life through death is one of the profoundest paradoxes in both the Christian faith and the Christian life.

Both life and death have always fascinated human beings. There can be no doubt that we are alive and that we will die. Life and death are two incontrovertible facts with which we have to come to terms. But they are also mysteries and hard to define.

Let me give you an example from a sphere of experience
of interest to me, namely ornithology.

*Life through death is one
of the profoundest paradoxes
in both the Christian faith
and the Christian life.*

Roger Tory Peterson, who died in 1997, was the doyen
of twentieth-century American birdwatchers and bird
artists. He used to tell how he got started. On a walk in
the country at the age of eleven he spotted a Flicker (a
species of Woodpecker). It appeared to be just a bundle of
brown feathers, clinging to the trunk of an oak tree.

> Gingerly I touched it on the back. Instantly this inert thing
> jerked its head around, looked at me with startled eyes, then
> exploded in a flash of golden wings, and fled into the wood.
> It was like a resurrection – what had appeared to be dead was
> very much alive. Ever since, birds have seemed to me the most
> vivid expression of life . . . Birds are an affirmation of life.[1]

Elsewhere Peterson described this as 'the crucial moment
of my life'. 'I was overwhelmed,' he continued, 'by the

contrast between something that was suddenly so vital and something I had taken for dead.'[2]

My concern in this chapter, however, is not with life and death in nature, but rather with death and life in Christ. The radical biblical perspective is to see death not as the termination of life but as the gateway to life.

For what Scripture does is to set before us the desirable glories of life, and then insist that the indispensable condition of experiencing them is death. In short, the Bible promises life *through* death, and it promises life on no other terms. So the apostle Paul describes Christian people as 'those who have been brought from death to life' (Romans 6:13). This perspective is so different from the assumptions of the secular mind, so novel, so revolutionary in its implications, that we need to see it illustrated in the six different situations in which according to the New Testament it operates.

SALVATION

First of all, we see death and life in relation to our salvation. For salvation is often represented in terms of life. Paul wrote that God's gift is eternal life (Romans 6:23), and John explained that those who have the Son have life (1 John 5:12). It's also made clear that the distinctive feature of this life is not its eternity but its quality as the life of the new age. Eternal life is life lived in fellowship with God (John 17:3).

But the only way to enter this life is death. The reason for this is clear. It is that the barrier to fellowship with God is sin, and 'the wages of sin is death' (Romans 6:23). Throughout the Bible sin and death are coupled together as an offence and its just penalty. But if we were to die for our own sins, that would be the end of us. There could be no life that way.

So God came to us in Jesus Christ. He took our place, bore our sin and died our death. We had sinned. So we deserved to die. But he died instead of us. The simple statement 'Christ died for sins' is enough. He had no sins of his own for which he needed to die; he died for ours.

But his death cannot do us any good unless we claim its benefits for ourselves. It is by faith inwardly and by baptism outwardly that we become united to Christ in his death and resurrection. We have died and risen with him. Now therefore we must 'count [or 'reckon'] ourselves dead to sin but alive to God in Christ Jesus' (Romans 6:11) – not pretending we are immune to sin when we know we are not, but realizing and remembering the fact that, being one with Christ, the benefits of his death have become ours. We are 'alive to God', alive through his death.

DISCIPLESHIP

The same principle of life through death operates in discipleship as in salvation. Jesus himself used this vivid symbolism:

Then he called the crowd to him along with his disciples and said: 'Whoever wants to be my disciple must deny themselves and take up their cross and follow me. For whoever wants to save their life will lose it, but whoever loses their life for me and for the gospel will save it (Mark 8:34–35).

If we had lived under Roman occupation in Palestine, and if we had seen a man carrying a cross, or at least the *patibulum* or crossbar, we would not have needed to ask him what on earth he was doing. No, we would have recognized him immediately as a condemned criminal on his way to execution, for the Romans compelled those they sentenced to death to carry their cross to the site of crucifixion.

This then was the dramatic imagery Jesus used for self-denial. For if we are following Jesus, there is only one place to which we can be going, the place of death. As Dietrich Bonhoeffer wrote in *The Cost of Discipleship*:[3] 'When Christ calls a man, he bids him come and die.' What is more, according to Luke we are to take up our cross every day (Luke 9:23), and if we do not do so we cannot be his disciple (Luke 14:27).

This teaching comes into direct collision with the Human Potential Movement, and with the New Age Movement too, which has jumped on the bandwagon of the Human Potential Movement. Carl Rogers taught that human beings are characterized not by pathology (as Freud taught) but by potential, and Abraham Maslow emphasized the need for self-actualization. Jesus' words about 'saving' and 'losing' our 'life', although they can certainly be applied to martyrdom, are not necessarily restricted to it. For our 'life' is our *psychē*, our self, and in other versions of this saying the reflexive is used, namely 'yourself'. So we could paraphrase verse 35: 'Whoever is determined to hold on to themselves and live for themselves, will lose themselves. But whoever is willing to die, to lose themselves, to give themselves away in the service of Christ and the gospel, will (in the moment of complete abandon) find themselves, and discover their true identity.' So Jesus does promise true self-discovery at the cost of self-denial, true life at the cost of death.

This teaching of Jesus was elaborated by the apostle Paul. In Galatians he declared that he had been crucified with Christ (2:20), and that all who belong to Christ have crucified their fallen nature with all its passions and desires (5:24). This is 'mortification', that is, putting to death or repudiating our fallen, self-indulgent nature. Paul's clearest statement of it is Romans 8:13:

> For if you live according to the sinful nature, you will die; but if by the Spirit you put to death the misdeeds of the body, you will live.

Here is a verse which draws a clear contrast between life and death. It affirms that there is a kind of life which actually leads to death, and there is also a kind of death which actually leads to life. So if we want to live a life of true fulfilment, we must put to death (radically reject) all evil. As Martyn Lloyd-Jones wrote:

> I am more and more convinced that most people get into trouble in the living of the Christian life because of their molly-coddling of themselves spiritually.[4]

Conversely if we reject evil, we will live. The only way to enter into the fullness of life is to die, or better to put to death, even to crucify, that is utterly to renounce, our self-indulgent nature and all its desires.

The Puritan John Owen emphasized this in his treatise *The Mortification of Sin in Believers* (1656). 'Hatred of sin as sin, not only as galling or disquieting,' he wrote, ' . . . lies at the bottom of all true spiritual mortification' (chapter 8). So it is essential to make war against indwelling sin and not to come to terms with it. We must avoid the 'great evil of speaking peace groundlessly to ourselves' (chapter 13). Moreover, such thoroughgoing mortification is possible only through the Holy Spirit. 'A man may easier see without eyes, or speak without a tongue, than truly mortify one sin without the Spirit' (chapter 7).

MISSION

The third area in which the life-through-death principle operates is mission. Although suffering is an indispensable aspect of mission, it is frequently overlooked. We need therefore to grasp its biblical basis before considering some notable examples of it.

Take the marvellous profile of the servant of the Lord in Isaiah chapters 42 – 53. His calling is to bring the light of salvation to the nations, but first he must endure mockery and persecution. Again, before he can 'sprinkle many nations' he will be despised and rejected by others, and will pour out his life unto death.

Douglas Webster, in his book *Yes to Mission*, gave an eloquent exposition of this theme:

> Mission sooner or later leads into passion. In biblical categories . . . the servant must suffer . . . it is this which makes mission effective . . . Every form of mission leads to some form of cross. The very shape of mission is cruciform. We can understand mission only in terms of the Cross . . .[5]

Jesus clearly saw himself as fulfilling the suffering servant prophecies, and spoke of the necessary place of suffering in mission. When a delegation of Greeks came to Philip with their request to see Jesus, Jesus replied:

> The hour has come for the Son of Man to be glorified [on the cross]. Very truly I tell you, unless a grain of wheat falls to the ground and dies, it remains only a single seed. But if it dies, it produces many seeds. Those who love their life will lose it, while those who hate their life in this world will keep it for eternal life (John 12:23–25).

Here again, although now in the context of mission rather than discipleship, Jesus uses the language of life and death, and emphasizes that death is the way to life. Only through his death would the gospel be extended to the Gentile world. Death is the way to fruitfulness. Unless it dies, the seed remains alone. But if it dies, it multiplies. It was so for the Messiah: it is the same for the Messiah's community, for 'whoever serves me must follow me' (John 12:26).

The biblical basis for mission suffering would be incomplete without reference to the apostle Paul. Consider this extraordinary statement of his:

So then, death is at work in us, but life is at work in you (2 Corinthians 4:12).

Here the apostle dares to claim that through his death others will live. Is he out of his mind? No! Does he really mean it? Yes! It is not, of course, that his own sufferings and death can bring about salvation, as does the suffering and death of Jesus Christ. It is rather this. People receive life through the gospel, and those who preach the gospel faithfully suffer for it. Paul knew what he was talking about. The good news he proclaimed was that salvation is available to Jews and Gentiles on equal terms, by faith alone. This aroused fanatical opposition from the Jews – so much so that it is no exaggeration to say that the Gentiles owed their salvation to his willingness to preach it faithfully and suffer for it. He was ready to die in order that they might live.

The history of the Christian church has been adorned by brave missionaries who risked their lives for the sake of the gospel, and who saw the church growing as a result. I will mention only two examples – one relating to an individual, and the other to a whole country.

The individual is Adoniram Judson of Burma (now Myanmar). When he proposed to his wife Ann, he said to her: 'Give me your hand to go with me to the jungles of Asia, and there die with me in the cause of Christ.' They reached Rangoon in 1813 and immediately soaked themselves in Burmese language and culture. Only after six years did Adoniram feel able to preach his first sermon, and only after seven could they register their first convert. It took him twenty years to translate the whole Bible into Burmese. He also wrote tracts, a catechism, a grammar and an English-Burmese dictionary which is still in use.

His sufferings were intense. He was widowed twice and lost six children during his lifetime. He and his family were constantly plagued with illness. During the Anglo-Burmese war he was suspected of being a spy and spent nearly two years in prison enduring chains, heat and filth. And in thirty-seven years of missionary service he returned home to the United States only once.

Yet as a result of his 'death and burial' in Burmese soil he bore much fruit. When he and Ann arrived in Burma, on their first Sunday in 1813 they shared in the Lord's

Supper together because there were no other Christians to invite to the table. When he died thirty-seven years later in 1850, however, he left more than 7,000 baptized Burmans and Karens in sixty-three churches. And now it is reckoned that there are more than three million Christians in Burma.

My second example relates to the vast country of China. When the Communists took over, and all foreign missionaries had to leave, it is believed that there were nearly one million Protestant Christians. Today the guess is that there are about seventy million.[6] How can we account for this? Tony Lambert has written as follows:

> The reason for the growth of the church in China and for the outbreak of genuine spiritual revival in many areas is inextricably linked to the whole theology of the cross . . . The stark message of the Chinese church is that God uses suffering and the preaching of a crucified Christ to pour out revival and build his church. Are we in the West still willing to hear? . . . The Chinese church . . . has walked the way of the cross. The lives and deaths of the martyrs of the 1950s and 1960s have borne rich fruit.[7]

The 'death' we are called to die as the condition of fruitfulness may well be less dramatic than martyrdom. Nevertheless, it is a real death, especially for cross-cultural missionaries. It may be for them a death to comfort and ease, and a separation from home and relatives; or a death to personal ambition as they renounce the temptation to climb the professional ladder, being content to remain in a humble servant ministry instead; or a death to cultural imperialism, refusing to exalt their inherited culture (despite it being part of their identity) and identifying instead with the culture of their adoption. In these and other ways we may be called to 'die' as the means to a life of fruitfulness.

PERSECUTION

The fourth area in which death is found to be the way to life is physical persecution.

Once again an outstanding example of this was the apostle Paul. Few Christians have suffered as he did – flogged, stoned, imprisoned, lynched and shipwrecked. Indeed, so extreme was the brutal treatment he received that he sometimes described it as a kind of 'death', and his deliverance from it as a kind of 'resurrection'. 'I die every day,' he wrote in the middle of his great chapter on resurrection (1 Corinthians 15:31, NIV), meaning that he was continuously exposed to the danger of death. Here is his fullest statement:

> We do not want you to be uninformed, brothers and sisters, about the troubles we experienced in the province of Asia. We were under great pressure, far beyond our ability to endure, so that we despaired of life itself. Indeed, we felt we had received the sentence of death. But this happened that

we might not rely on ourselves but on God, who raises the dead. He has delivered us from such a deadly peril, and he will deliver us again. On him we have set our hope that he will continue to deliver us (2 Corinthians 1:8–10).

By no means all beleaguered Christians are repeatedly rescued from death as Paul was. Christians are promised neither immunity nor deliverance. Instead, even in the midst of death we can experience life.

We always carry around in our body the death of Jesus, so that the life of Jesus may also be revealed in our body. For we who are alive are always being given over to death for Jesus' sake, so that his life may also be revealed in our mortal body (2 Corinthians 4:10–11).

This extraordinary statement declares that we can experience both the death and the life of Jesus simultaneously. Notice that the noun 'body' and the adverb 'always' are repeated in verses 10 and 11. We are always sharing in our body in the death and the life of Jesus. Even while we are being afflicted physically, and made aware of our mortality, we can draw on the spiritual vitality of Jesus. Even before the resurrection takes place we experience the resurrection-life of Jesus. Thus 'dying, and yet we live on' (2 Corinthians 6:9).

Whatever Paul's thorn in the flesh was (some think it was sickness, others persecution), it was certainly a physical problem of some kind. And although Paul cried out for deliverance, he was promised instead Christ's power in his weakness. Indeed the truth at the core of Paul's letters to the church in Corinth is power through weakness, glory through suffering and life through death.

In the end Paul was not delivered but executed. He sealed his witness with his blood. And in the final book of the Bible the people of God are warned of persecution and martyrdom. Jesus told the church in Smyrna: 'Do not be afraid of what you are about to suffer . . . Be faithful, even to the point of death, and I will give you life as your victor's crown' (Revelation 2:10).

Dr Paul Marshall of the Institute of Christian Studies in Toronto writes in his book *Their Blood Cries Out* about 'the worldwide tragedy of modern Christians who are dying for their faith'. He calculates that 200 million Christians worldwide live in daily fear of the secret police under state repression. In more than sixty countries worldwide Christians are harassed, abused, imprisoned, tortured and executed, simply on account of their faith. Yet 'despite persecution, Christianity is growing rapidly in the world'.[8]

MARTYRDOM

In my treatment of the theme of 'life through death' it will be noted that I am separating martyrdom from persecution. This is not because I have failed to notice that they overlap (which they do) but because according to Scripture,

a special honour will be accorded to them in the new world
(see Revelation 20:4).

So I begin in this section by introducing you to Dr Josif
Ton, a follower of Jesus Christ, who has shown by his
life and teaching that suffering – and even death – is an
indispensable ingredient of Christian discipleship. Josif
Ton is a Romanian Christian leader, born in 1934, who
became pastor of the Baptist Church in Oradea, which
today is a world-famous Baptist Centre. After four years
of faithful pastoring, the curiosity of the authorities was
aroused and he was arrested and interrogated. He was then
given the opportunity to leave the country and settle
in the USA, where he pursued doctoral studies and was
awarded a doctorate by the Evangelical Faculty of Belgium.
His research topic was 'Suffering, Martyrdom and Rewards
in Heaven' which was later published as a book.

During the oppressive regime of Nicolae Ceauşescu,
Josif Ton in one of his published sermons told how the
authorities threatened to kill him. He responded: 'Sir,
your supreme weapon is killing. My supreme weapon is
dying.'

One who was 'faithful unto death' was Dietrich Bonhoeffer.
He was imprisoned in the Flossenburg concentration camp.
On Sunday, 8th April, 1945 he led a short service of
worship. He had hardly finished his last prayer when the
door opened and two men in civilian clothes came in and
said: 'Prisoner Bonhoeffer, get ready to come with us.'
Those words 'come with us' had come for all prisoners to

mean one thing only – the scaffold. 'This is the end,' he said, 'for me the beginning of life'.[9]

MORTALITY

So far we have considered five areas in which death is the way to life. We have seen it in salvation (Christ died that we might live), in discipleship (if we put to death the misdeeds of the body we will live), in mission (the seed must die to multiply), in persecution (dying that we may live) and in martyrdom. Now, however, in this section, we will face our mortality, and the death of our physical body. Having at the time of writing by the grace of God reached the age of eighty-eight, my readers will understand that I have been reflecting much about these things. The end is in sight. I have been encouraged by the paradox of life through death.

Death inspires terror in many people
. . . But death holds no horrors
for Christians.

Death inspires terror in many people. Woody Allen's *angst* in relation to death is well known. He sees it as a total annihilation of being and finds it 'absolutely stupefying in its terror'. 'It's not that I'm afraid to die,' he quips, 'I just don't want to be there when it happens.'[10]

Another and similar example is given by Ronald Dworkin QC, the American legal philosopher, who has held chairs in London, Oxford and New York universities. He has written:

> Death's central horror is oblivion – the terrifying absolute dying of the light . . . Death has dominion because it is not only the start of nothing, but the end of everything . . .[11]

But death holds no horrors for Christians. True, the process of dying can be messy and undignified, and the decay which follows it is not pleasant. Indeed the Bible itself recognizes this by calling death 'the last enemy to be destroyed' (1 Corinthians 15:26). At the same time we affirm that 'Christ Jesus . . . has destroyed death' (2 Timothy 1:10). He has personally conquered it by his resurrection, so that it no longer has any authority over us. Consequently we can shout defiantly:

> Where, O death, is your victory?
>   Where, O death, is your sting?
> (1 Corinthians 15:55)

The defeat of death is one thing; the gift of life is another. But because of the difficulty of defining eternal life, the

New Testament writers tend to resort to picture language. The apostle John, for example, describes the people of God as having their names inscribed in the book of life (Revelation 3:5; 21:27), enjoying continuous access to the tree of life (Revelation 2:7; 22:2), and drinking freely of the water of life (Revelation 7:17; 21:6; 22:1, 17).

'But someone will ask, "How are the dead raised? With what kind of body will they come?"' (1 Corinthians 15:35). The same question (a foolish question, according to Paul) is frequently asked today. We answer it by drawing attention to the relationship between a seed and its flower. There will be an essential continuity between the two (e.g. mustard seeds produce only a mustard plant). But the discontinuity is much more striking. The seed is bare and ugly but its flower is colourful and beautiful. So will it be with our resurrection body. It will preserve a degree of continuity with our present body, but it will have new and undreamed-of powers (1 Corinthians 15:35–44).

Furthermore, what is true of the resurrection body will in some way apply to the new heaven and new earth. Jesus called it a 'regeneration' (*palingenesia*, Matthew 19:28). For if the body is to be resurrected, the world is to be regenerated. And as there is to be a blend of continuity and discontinuity between the two bodies, so surely will there be between the two worlds. The whole creation is going to be liberated from its bondage to decay (Romans 8:18–25). These great expectations will be part of the eternal life into which death will bring us. It is this which is proclaimed in many cemeteries and on many tombstones: *Mors janua vitae*, death is the gateway to life.

Reflecting on death and seeking to prepare for it, I have constantly returned to what one might call Paul's philosophy of life and death:

> For to me, to live is Christ and to die is gain. If I am to go on living in the body, this will mean fruitful labour for me. Yet what shall I choose? I do not know! I am torn between the two: I desire to depart and be with Christ, which is better by far (Philippians 1:21–23).

In one word, life meant Christ to Paul. He could not imagine life without him. So it was truly logical that he should want to die because death would bring gain, namely more of Christ. Nevertheless, he knew he would remain a while longer because there was more work for him to do on earth.

It is usually regarded as dangerous to argue from an analogy. But Paul here seems to give us permission to do so. The principle is clear. If life means Christ to us, then death will bring gain. Indeed the life to come will be 'far better' than life on earth.

For example,

- If worship with God's people on earth is profoundly satisfying (which it is), then worship with all in heaven will be more thrilling still.

- If our heart burns within us whenever the Scriptures are opened to us, all truth will be even more moving.
- If the glory of a sunset stirs us now, what will the beauty of the new heaven and earth be like?
- If cross-cultural fellowship moves us now, the great crowds from every nation of tribe and language will cause us to rejoice when we all finally come together.
- If sometimes we have known what it is to 'rejoice with joy unspeakable, and full of glory', we shall expect it more often there where there will be neither sorrow nor tears.

These are only samples of human experience. In each case it is appropriate to use the comparative, namely 'better by far'. Indeed, when we reflect on the life to come, the comparative is really inadequate and the superlative is appropriate. This is why, whenever we are reflecting on the future that awaits us, we can always say, 'The best is yet to come.'

To recap, in this chapter we have looked at six areas where we find the paradoxical principle of life through death: salvation, discipleship, mission, persecution, martyrdom and mortality. In each case we must maintain both sides of the equation, death and life.

On the one hand we must not understate the glory of the life which is offered us in the gospel – the eternal life which is ours through faith in Christ, or the intensified life which is ours if we put to death the desires of our fallen

nature, or the inward vitality we can enjoy in the midst of
our physical weakness and mortality, or the fruitfulness
promised to those who are faithful in their mission, or the
comfort given us in the midst of persecution and in prospect
of martyrdom, or – most of all – the final resurrection-life
in the new creation. In all these ways God has promised
that those who die will live.

On the other hand, we must not understate the cost of
the death which alone leads to life – a death to sin through
identification with Christ, a death to self as we follow
Christ, a death to ambition in cross-cultural mission, a
death to security in the experience of persecution and one
of martyrdom, and a death to this world as we prepare for
our final destiny.

Death is unnatural and unpleasant. In one sense it
presents us with a terrible finality. Death is the end. Yet in
every situation death is the way to life. So if we want to
live we must die. And we will be willing to die only when
we see the glories of the life to which death leads. This is
the radical, paradoxical Christian perspective. Truly Christian people are accurately described as 'those who are alive
from the dead'.

CONCLUSION

We have considered eight characteristics of those who desire to follow Jesus, and which together form my portrait of the radical disciple.

To be sure, I have been selective and my selection has been somewhat arbitrary. Yet there are aspects of discipleship which I would like to see in every disciple of Jesus, and not least in myself.

You will no doubt want to compile your own list. Hopefully it will be clearly biblical, but still also reflect your own culture and experience, and I wish you well as you do so.

We cannot conclude better than to hear and heed the words of Jesus in the upper room:

> You call me 'Teacher' and 'Lord', and rightly so, for that is what I am (John 13:13).

Basic to all discipleship is our resolve not only to address Jesus with polite titles, but to follow his teaching and obey his commands.

POSTSCRIPT: FAREWELL!

As I lay down my pen for the last time (literally, since I confess I am not computerized) at the age of eighty-eight, I venture to send this valedictory message to my readers. I am grateful for your encouragement, for many of you have written to me.

Looking ahead, none of us of course knows what the future of printing and publishing may be. But I myself am confident that the future of books is assured and that, though they will be complemented, they will never be altogether replaced. For there is something unique about books. Our favourite books become very precious to us and we even develop with them an almost living and affectionate relationship. Is it an altogether fanciful fact that we handle, stroke and even smell them as tokens of our esteem and affection? I am not referring only to an author's feeling for what he has written, but to all readers and their library. I have made it a rule not to quote from any book unless I have first handled it. So let me urge you to keep reading, and encourage your relatives and friends to do the same. For this is a much-neglected means of grace.

Of course, there are millions of our sisters and brothers in Christ around the world who would dearly love to have books to read to help them grow in their discipleship. Yet they have almost none, while we in the West have more than anybody can read. That is why I have assigned the royalties of all my own books to the work of Langham Literature, to enable more believers and their pastors in poorer parts of the world to obtain good Christian books both in English and in their own languages, and so be strengthened in their faith and their preaching. I wonder if I might encourage you to consider this and the other ministries of the Langham Partnership, which are dear to my own heart, as worthy of your interest and support.

Readers may like to know that I have appointed in my will a small group of literary executors chaired by Frank Entwistle, who are kindly willing to handle any questions which may arise in relation to my books. A sample of each book, together with a sample of contributions to other books and all my papers, will be kept in safe custody in Lambeth Palace Library by generous agreement of Dr Richard Palmer, the librarian and archivist, who has kindly offered to make them available to researchers. My office address will continue to be 12 Weymouth Street, London W1W 5BY and will be supervised by Frances Whitehead, the inimitable and indefatigable.

Once again, farewell!

NOTES

Preface
1. Matthew 13:3–23; Mark 4:3–20; Luke 8:4–15.
2. 'Come, let us join our cheerful songs', Isaac Watts (1674–1748).

Chapter 1
1. Transaction Publishers, 1955, p. 16.

Chapter 2
1. For more information on the Keswick Convention, the most recent and resourceful history is: Ian M. Randall and Charles Price, *Transforming Keswick: The Keswick Convention, Past, Present and Future* (Paternoster Press, 2000).
2. Michael Ramsay, *Images Old and New* (SPCK, 1963), p. 14.
3. Lutterworth Press, 1972.

Chapter 3
1. Hodder & Stoughton, 3rd edition, 2005.

Chapter 4
1. IVP, 2000.
2. IVP, 1984.
3. Adapted with permission from my Foreword to *The Care of Creation*. Two useful recent books on the subject are R. J. Berry (ed.), *When Enough is Enough: A Christian Framework for Environmental Sustainability* (Apollos, 2007) and Dave Bookless, *Planetwise: Dare to Care for God's World* (IVP, 2008).
4. '1 billion' is used in the UK to mean a million millions. But now it is an almost universal cipher for a thousand millions.
5. Sphere, 1973.
6. For the contents of this chapter see Chapter 5, 'Caring for Creation' in John Stott, *Issues Facing Christians Today* (Zondervan, 4th edition, 2006), thoroughly updated by Roy McCloughry.
7. Monarch Books, 2008.
8. Peter Harris, *Under the Bright Wings* (Regent College Publishing, 2000); *Kingfisher's Fire* (Monarch, 2008).
9. This and the following quotations are taken from Chris Wright, *The Mission of God* (IVP, 2008).
10. Quoted from John Stott, Foreword to *The Care of Creation*.

Chapter 6
1. *The First Epistle of St Peter* (Macmillan, 1961, 2nd edition).
2. Orval Hobart Mowrer, 1907–82.

Chapter 7

1. Matthew 6:9–13; Luke 11:2–4.
2. *The Christian Priest Today* (SPCK 1972, revised edition 1985), from chapter 11, 'Divine Humility', pp. 79–91.
3. HarperCollins paperback, 1957.
4. Translated by Edwin Hudson from the French (SCM Press Ltd, 1972), pp. 11, 40, 43.

Chapter 8

1. Alice E. Mace (ed.), *The Birds Around Us* (Ortho Books, 1986). From the introductory chapter by Roger Tory Peterson entitled 'The Joy of Birds', pp. 19–20.
2. William Zinsser, 'A Field Guide to Roger Tory Peterson' in *Audubon* vol. 94, No. 6, p. 93.
3. First published in English in 1948 (SCM Press).
4. D. M. Lloyd-Jones, *Romans 6: The New Man* (Banner of Truth, 1992), his comment on verse 19, p. 264.
5. Douglas Webster, *Yes to Mission* (SCM, 1966), pp. 101–102.
6. *Operation World* estimates a figure of 69.2 million for Christian church members in China, but adds that accurate statistics are not available. See Patrick Johnstone and Jason Mandryk, *Operation World* (Paternoster, 2001), p. 160.
7. Tony Lambert, *The Resurrection of the Chinese Church* (Hodder, 1991), pp. 174 and 267.
8. Paul Marshall with Lela Gilbert, *Their Blood Cries Out* (W. Publishing Group, Thomas Nelson, 1997), p. 8.

9. Dietrich Bonhoeffer, from the Foreword to *Letters and Papers from Prison* (Fontana, 1959), p. 11.

10. From an article in *Esquire*, 1977. And in Graham McCann, *Woody Allen, New Yorker* (Polity Press, 1990), pp. 43 and 83.

11. Ronald Dworkin, *Life's Dominion* (HarperCollins, 1993), p. 199.